Presented to
The
Fairhope Public
Library

In Memory
of
Nancy Cain

By
Bluestocking Book Club
2014

EYEWITNESS TRAVEL

Left **Allerdale Ramble** Centre **St Michael's, Hawkshead** Right **Dora's Field**

LONDON, NEW YORK,
MELBOURNE, MUNICH AND DELHI
www.dk.com

Printed and bound in China by
South China Printing Company

First American Edition, 2011
13 14 15 16 10 9 8 7 6 5 4 3 2 1

Published in the United States by
Dorling Kindersley Limited, 80 Strand, London
WC2R 0RL, UK

**Copyright 2013 © Dorling Kindersley Limited,
London, A Penguin Company**

Floors are referred to throughout in accordance
with European usage; ie the "first floor" is the
floor above ground level.

Published in Great Britain by Dorling
Kindersley Limited

ISSN 1479-344X

ISBN 978 0 7566 9633 7

Within each Top 10 list in this book, no hierarchy
of quality or popularity is implied. All 10 are, in the
editor's opinion, of roughly equal merit.

MIX
Paper from
responsible sources
FSC™ C018179

Contents

The Lake District's Top 10

The information in this DK Eyewitness Top 10 Travel Guide is checked regularly.
Every effort has been made to ensure that this book is as up-to-date as possible at the time of
going to press. Some details, however, such as telephone numbers, opening hours, prices,
gallery hanging arrangements and travel information are liable to change. The publishers
cannot accept responsibility for any consequences arising from the use of this book, nor for
any material on third party websites, and cannot guarantee that any website address in this
book will be a suitable source of travel information. We value the views and suggestions of
our readers very highly. Please write to: Publisher, DK Eyewitness Travel Guides,
Dorling Kindersley, 80 Strand, London WC2R 0RL, UK, or email travelguides@uk.dk.com

Left **Grasmere** Centre **Hardknott Pass** Right **Townend**

Around the Lake District

Streetsmart

Left **Ambleside** Right **Windermere**

Key to abbreviations
Adm *admission charge*

THE LAKE DISTRICT'S TOP 10

THE LAKE DISTRICT'S TOP 10

TOP 10 The Lake District's Highlights

The Lake District is one of the most beautiful and romantic parts of Britain, with spectacular mountains, verdant valleys and, of course, plenty of lakes. It is a terrific place for outdoor activities – by evening every country pub is playing host to recuperating hikers. The district was put on the tourist map by Wordsworth, and it has long been accustomed to providing hearty food, real ale and a comfortable bed for visitors. Wild it may be, but domestic pleasures are always reassuringly close at hand in the Lakes.

1 Grasmere

Pretty Grasmere village is an enchanting destination, circled by high fells and isolated tarns, and replete with teashops and handsome stone cottages. Wordsworth's famous Dove Cottage is just a short walk away *(see pp8–9)*.

2 Windermere

Taking a cruise on England's largest lake is a must. The surrounding area is rich in historic homes, such as Blackwell and Townend *(see pp10–12)*.

3 Kendal

The gateway town to the Lake District, Kendal features an exceptional art gallery, a fine museum, some good restaurants and a lively arts centre *(see pp12–13)*.

4 Borrowdale

Lush and thickly wooded, Borrowdale is scattered with wonderful stone farmhouses and pretty villages, many in the shadow of high fells *(see pp14–15)*.

Preceding pages **Rock garden, Sizergh Castle, Kendal**

Ambleside
5 Centrally located and with a bustling air, this little town makes an excellent base for a holiday in the Lakes (see pp16–17).

The Langdale Valley
6 With high mountains, tumbling waterfalls, country pubs and hiking opportunities galore, Langdale should not be missed (see pp18–19).

Wordsworth's Lake District
7 The area is scattered with walks, houses and views associated with the poet Wordsworth and his sister Dorothy, whose journals inspired some of his best poems (see pp20–23).

Conlston Water
8 Elongated Coniston Water was Arthur Ransome's inspiration for the much loved *Swallows and Amazons* children's books; as a child, he spent his holidays at Nibthwaite, which sits at the lake's southern end (see pp24–5).

Wasdale
9 One of the remotest and most scenic parts of the area, where you can go for hikes, stay in a tent or at Wasdale Head Inn (see pp26–7).

Keswick
10 A workday town in the northern Lake District, but one with terrific museums, markets, theatres and amenities. Keswick also has some iconic walks, as well as Derwent Water, nearby (see pp28–9).

Share your travel recommendations on **traveldk.com**

🔟 Grasmere

Sitting in the middle of the Central Fells, Grasmere, with its handsome stone cottages and lush surroundings, is the archetypal Lake District settlement. Home to Wordsworth and his extended family for five years, the village features all the pleasures of the region rolled into one. There are rugged walks to isolated tarns and peaks, watersports on Grasmere lake, an early medieval church and a range of independent shops and galleries. And of course, this being the Lakes, a cream tea or a pint is always close by.

Interior of Jumble Room

🔵 **The colourful Jumble Room on Langdale Road is a fun choice for dinner.**

• Map E5
• *Sarah Nelson's Gingerbread Shop: Church Cottage; 015394 35428; open 9:15am–5:30pm Mon–Sat, 12:30–5:30pm Sun; www. grasmeregingerbread. co.uk*
• *The Wordsworth Museum and Art Gallery: southeast of Grasmere; 015394 35544; open 9:30am–5pm (4pm in winter), closed Jan; adm £7.50; www.wordsworth.org.uk*
• *Heaton Cooper Studio: The Green; 015394 35280; open 9am–5:30pm Mon–Sat, 11am–5pm Sun; www. heatoncooper.co.uk*
• *Dove Cottage: southeast of Grasmere; 015394 35544; open 9:30am–5pm (4pm in winter), closed Jan; adm £7.50; www. wordsworth.org.uk*
• *Sam Read's Bookshop: Broadgate House; 015394 35374*

Top 10 Features

1. Sarah Nelson's Gingerbread Shop
2. The Wordsworth Museum and Art Gallery
3. The Coffin Trail
4. Dove Cottage
5. Greenhead Ghyll
6. Heaton Cooper Studio
7. Hike to Easedale Tarn
8. Rowing on the Lake
9. St Oswald's Church
10. Sam Read's Bookshop

1 Sarah Nelson's Gingerbread Shop

The warm, spicy smell of gingerbread – made to a secret recipe since the mid-19th century – will lead you to this shop *(below)* next to the churchyard. Housed in a quaint cottage, it is staffed by a maiden in a mob cap.

The Coffin Trail

The name refers to the fact that this route *(right)*, which takes you above the valley floor from Grasmere to Rydal then Ambleside, was used by coffin bearers taking bodies from Rydal for burial at St Oswald's. It is a lovely stretching walk.

2 The Wordsworth Museum and Art Gallery

One of the best museums in the Lakes, with portraits of Wordsworth and his contemporaries (including a swooningly handsome Byron), letters, and fascinating memorabilia. Headphones allow you to tune in to poetry readings.

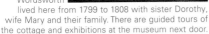

Dove Cottage

Wordsworth lived here from 1799 to 1808 with sister Dorothy, wife Mary and their family. There are guided tours of the cottage and exhibitions at the museum next door.

Greenhead Ghyll

Just east of the village, a signed path leads you along Greenhead Ghyll, which features in Wordsworth's *Michael* as "the tumultuous brook of Greenhead Ghyll". The enticing path leads up to Alcock Tarn.

Heaton Cooper Studio

This gallery has been run by the Heaton Cooper family since 1905 and features the paintings of Alfred and William Heaton Cooper, as well as prints and sculptures.

Hike to Easedale Tarn

A signed path *(above)* leads northwest from the village for the three-hour round trip to Easedale Tarn, a lake ringed by magnificent peaks and crags. A steep but satisfying hike.

Rowing on the Lake

Rent a boat at the Faeryland Tea Garden just south of the village to experience some wonderful views of the surrounding fells. Then return to Faeryland for a cup of tea and some cake (summer only).

St Oswald's Church

At the heart of Grasmere is the bulky church of St Oswald *(above)*, which has a 13th-century nave and a timber roof. The Wordsworths are buried in the graveyard.

Sam Read's Bookshop

This great little shop *(left)* has a wide range of local publications, a strong fiction section and lots of books for kids. The owner is likely to have read any title you ask about.

De Quincey in Grasmere

Thomas de Quincey, author of *Confessions of an English Opium Eater* (1821), came to stay with the Wordsworths in Grasmere in 1809. He had been addicted to opium since the tender age of 19, having first taken it in the form of laudanum to ease toothache. When the Wordsworths moved to Allan Bank, de Quincey took over Dove Cottage, and his relationship with the poet, who he had admired to the point of adulation, began to cool.

⁀10 Windermere

The lakeside town of Windermere is a transport hub for the region due to its railway station; Windermere also has the railway to thank for the grey stone guesthouses and impressive villas that were built in the Victorian period. The town does not have the intimate feel of other Lake District settlements, but there are some superb hotels nearby, and the lake – England's largest – is wonderful to explore, by cruise, canoe or rowing boat. Some unique sights are dotted around the lake, chief among them Townend and Blackwell.

The Craft Shop, Blackwell

🍴 **Blackwell's tearoom is an elegant option for lunch.**

• Blackwell: Map N2; 015394 46139; 10.30am–5pm daily; adm £7.20
• Hill Top: Near Sawrey; Map M2; 015394 36269; mid-Mar–end-Oct: 10:30am–4:30pm Sat–Thu; adm £8; timed tickets • Lakeside & Haverthwaite Railway: S Windermere; Map M3; 015395 31594; £6.30 for an adult return • Windermere Steamboat Museum: Rayrigg Rd; Map N2; 015394 45565; closed for redevelopment • Fell Foot Park: Newby Bridge; Map N3; 015395 31273; summer: 9am–5pm
• Townend: S of Troutbeck; Map N1; 015394 32628; mid-Mar–Oct: 1–4pm Wed–Sun; adm £4.40 • Lake District Visitor Centre: Map N2; 015394 46601; Mar–Nov: 10am–5pm, Nov–Mar: 10am–4pm • Stott Park Bobbin Mill, Ulverston; Map N3; 015395 31087; Apr–Oct: 11am–5pm Mon–Fri; adm £6.20
• Lake Cruise: 015394 43360; adm £7.20–16.50

Top 10 Features

1. Blackwell
2. Hill Top
3. Lakeside & Haverthwaite Railway
4. Walk to Orrest Head
5. Windermere Steamboat Museum
6. Fell Foot Park
7. Townend
8. Lake District Visitor Centre
9. Stott Park Bobbin Mill
10. A Lake Cruise

1 Blackwell

With its clear bold lines, lofty oak timber-framed and galleried main hall, and elongated floral motifs on the tiles and furniture, Blackwell *(above)* is a jewel of the Arts and Crafts movement. It was built by M H Baillie-Scott as a holiday home for the industrialist Sir Edward Holt.

2 Hill Top

This 17th-century farmhouse is an absolute must-see for Beatrix Potter fans. The house-museum records her life and work and has plenty of memorabilia on display. Hill Top is also a beautiful spot in its own right, with a recreation of Mr McGregor's garden.

3 Lakeside & Haverthwaite Railway

The gleaming, quaint steam engines *(below)* of the Lakeside & Haverthwaite Railway chug all the way through the Leven Valley, making their way from Haverthwaite Station to Lakeside.

5 Windermere Steamboat Museum

The museum showcases a collection of the historic craft that have plied the lake, including *Dolly*, the world's oldest mechanically powered boat.

4 Walk to Orrest Head

Starting at the northern end of the town, the steep walk up to Orrest Head takes you high above the lake and offers magnificent views *(above)*.

6 Fell Foot Park

This National Trust-run park *(main image)* is a great location for watersports, picnics and viewing daffodils in early spring.

7 Townend

One of the area's most compelling sights is 17th-century Townend *(above)*. This rugged stone and slate building with round chimneys and a wooden interior was owned by the Browne family for centuries.

8 Lake District Visitor Centre

A great place for kids! The centre includes an adventure playground, a café, gardens, free indoor soft play area, tree top trek and boat hire.

9 Stott Park Bobbin Mill

The 19th-century bobbin mill provides an insight into the grim industrial past. There are guided tours for visitors.

10 A Lake Cruise

A cruise on Lake Windermere *(below)* is a must for visitors. Options range from short hops around nearby islands to jazz and buffet cruises.

The Cult of Beatrix Potter

Bowness-on-Windermere features a perennially popular attraction: The World of Beatrix Potter, with interactive activities and shopping opportunities. However, it is fair to say that this commercial endeavour might not have been approved by the author. Fans should visit Hill Top instead, or explore the fells on foot with one of her beautifully illustrated books as a companion.

TOP 10 Kendal

Although Kendal sits outside the boundaries of the national park, it is the introduction to the region for many visitors, as it is on the train line from Oxenholme. Indeed, the handsome little market town has many of the most appealing characteristics of the Lakes, in the form of fine stone buildings, independent shops and restaurants, and the verdant hills that surround it. The two unmissable attractions here are the excellent Abbot Hall Art Gallery and the absorbing Museum of Lakeland Life and Industry.

Exhibit, Brewery Arts Centre

🍽 **The Waterside Wholefood café by the river is one of Kendal's prettiest and best lunch options.**

• *Brewery Arts Centre: Highgate; Map S3; 01539 725133; 10am–8pm Mon–Sat; noon–8:30pm Sun*
• *Levens Hall: Map P3; 015395 60321; Easter–Oct: noon–5pm Sun–Thu; adm £12* • *Abbot Hall: Map T3, 01539 722464, combined ticket £8; Art Gallery: adm £6.20; Museum of Lakeland Life and Industry: 10:30am–5pm Mon–Sat, adm £5*
• *Sizergh Castle: Map P3; 015395 60951; Mar–Nov: 1–5pm Sun–Thu; adm £9* • *Kendal Museum: Station Road; Map T1; 01539 721374; 10:30am–5pm Wed–Sat;*
• *Low Sizergh Barn: Map P3; 015395 60426; 9am–5pm daily* • *The Lakeland Climbing Centre: Lake District Business Park; Map P2; 01539 721766; 10am–10pm Mon–Fri, 10am–7pm weekend*
• *Quaker Tapestry: Stramongate; Map T2; 01539 722975; Apr–Dec; 10am–5pm Mon–Sat; adm £7.50*

Top 10 Features

1. Brewery Arts Centre
2. Levens Hall
3. Walk to the Castle Ruins
4. Abbot Hall Art Gallery
5. Museum of Lakeland Life and Industry
6. Sizergh Castle
7. Low Sizergh Barn
8. Kendal Museum
9. The Lakeland Climbing Centre
10. Quaker Tapestry

1 Brewery Arts Centre

This cosmopolitan arts venue *(above)* features cinema screens, a theatre, exhibition space, a bar and a restaurant. It is housed in a dramatic terraced stone building that was originally a brewery.

2 Levens Hall

An imposing Elizabethan home, Levens Hall is decked with rich furnishings, oak panelling and leather wall-coverings, as well as what is thought to be the oldest topiary garden in the world.

3 Walk to the Castle Ruins

The circular stone walls *(above)* and tall towers of the 12th-century Kendal Castle are visible wherever you are in town. The steep but satisfying walk to the castle provides a pretty view of the town and surrounding countryside.

Museum of Lakeland Life and Industry

Engaging, educational and beautiful displays *(top left)* with a step-back-in-time feel: you can browse in Edwardian shops, peek into a lead mine and walk into the parlour of a Lakeland farm.

Abbot Hall Art Gallery

High-profile contemporary art shows are held at Abbot Hall *(above)*. The gallery also features a fine collection of works by local artist George Romney.

Sizergh Castle

This impressive building was extended in Elizabethan times; highlights include oak interiors and a limestone garden.

Low Sizergh Barn

Low Sizergh has a farmyard trail complete with pigs and chickens. The magnificent timbered barn features a grocery, a crafts outlet *(above)* and a fine café.

Kendal Museum

Wainwright himself once worked at Kendal Museum *(left)*. It boasts an intriguing collection, including local Roman and Viking finds and has displays on wildlife and natural history.

The Lakeland Climbing Centre

A well-run and enjoyable attraction, the climbing centre is a great diversion on a rainy day. Its 25-m (82-ft) high climbing wall provides good training for climbing real mountains.

Quaker Tapestry

This tapestry, housed at Kendal Meeting house *(right)*, consists of 77 colourful embroidered panels and interactive displays, which reveal a wealth of social history.

Kendal Mint Cake

Kendal is the home of the astonishingly sweet confection known as Kendal Mint Cake. The dense, sugary mint sometimes comes wrapped in chocolate. It is famous both for its tooth-rotting qualities, and for giving a boost to flagging fell-walkers. According to legend, it was invented as a result of a culinary accident. Kendal Mint Cake was first produced in the town in 1869.

TOP 10 Borrowdale

Lush and heavily wooded, the valley of Borrowdale has a distinctly otherwordly air, as befits its name, which could be straight out of a Tolkien novel. The trees seem to be taller than elsewhere, the crags higher, the fells soar above and the valley bottom is dense with huge ferns, yews and oaks. There are some lovely little villages clustered along the River Derwent, and you will find plenty of opportunities for fell walks, as well as watersports on nearby Derwent Water.

The Borrowdale Rambler

The regularity of the Borrowdale Rambler makes public transport a very good option here.

There is nowhere prettier for a cup of tea and cakes than the riverside Grange Bridge Tea Shop.

• Map D4
• Grange Bridge Tea Shop: 01768 777201

Top 10 Features

1. Grange-in-Borrowdale
2. Rosthwaite
3. The Bowderstone
4. Castle Crag
5. Derwent Water
6. Seatoller
7. Seathwaite
8. Stonethwaite
9. The Borrowdale Rambler
10. Allerdale Ramble

1 Grange-in-Borrowdale

The village *(above)*, built around a stone bridge over the Derwent, is an enchanting spot. There is little to do but enjoy the view and the scones at the Grange Bridge Tearoom *(see p97)*, and watch the water go by.

2 Rosthwaite

The whitewashed cottages of tiny Rosthwaite provide some of the most attractive accommodation in the region. If you are here on the first Saturday of August you will be in prime position for the Borrowdale Fell Race.

3 The Bowderstone

This giant stone *(below)* is a rather peculiar but mesmerizing attraction, thought to have been transported here from Scotland via a glacier. You can ascend it by a wooden ladder.

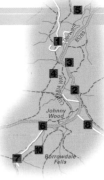

4 Castle Crag
A lovely walk from Grange up a peak that peers over the treetops and provides great views of Borrowdale, Castle Crag *(above)* may have been the site of an ancient fort, which explains the name.

5 Derwent Water
A footpath leads north from Grange-in-Borrowdale to the southern edge of the long and narrow Derwent Water, which is perfect for canoeing, kayaking, windsurfing and rowing.

6 Seatoller
A pretty hamlet *(left)* that is a good base for walkers, Seatoller is also the starting point of the bizarre annual manhunt inspired by Robert Louis Stevenson's *Kidnapped*, when runners chase each other over the fells.

7 Seathwaite
Sitting at the end of a country road, tiny Seathwaite *(right)* is the start of hiking routes up Scafell Pike and Great Gable. There is also a popular camp site here.

8 Stonethwaite
Another rugged little settlement, Stonethwaite lies on the route of the Cumbria Way *(see p18)*, providing accommodation for hikers in its white-washed cottages, and the 16th-century Langstrath Country Inn *(see p96)*.

9 The Borrowdale Rambler
Bus No. 78, more poetically known as the Borrowdale Rambler, is a great way of touring this beautiful part of the Lakes. The route winds itself through Borrowdale before culminating at Seatoller.

10 Allerdale Ramble
A long-distance walk covering 72–97 km (45–60 miles) depending on which route you take, the Allerdale Ramble *(above)* runs between Seathwaite and the Solway Firth, taking in gorgeous landscapes and dramatic seascapes.

Borrowdale Yews
Wordsworth wrote of four mighty yews near Seathwaite in Borrowdale in "Yew Trees" (1803). He described them as "those Fraternal Four of Borrowdale, joined in one solemn and capacious grove". One has fallen victim to a storm, but three gnarled and massive trees survive.

Ambleside

Ambleside is a terrific base for a holiday in the Lakes, if you are not just looking for outdoor activities. It has got an attractively sophisticated air for such a small place, with a couple of cinemas, cafés, bookshops and some excellent restaurants. Handy for accessing the northern shores of Windermere, it is also within easy reach of the stunning Langdale Valley (see pp18–19). If you need to stock up on camping, hiking or climbing gear this is the place to do it – there are innumerable outdoor stores here.

Zeffirelli's cinema

🚗 Parking in Ambleside is difficult and expensive, so it is easier to take a bus.

🍴 In general, the cafés and restaurants offer better food than the local pubs.

• Map F5
• St Mary's Parish Church: Vicarage Road
• Armitt Collection: Rydal Road; 015394 31212; open 10am–4:30pm Mon–Sat, adm £3.50
• Ambleside Climbing Wall: Lake Road; 015394 33794; open 10am–9:30pm Mon–Fri (to 8:30pm Sat &Sun); adm £7.50–8.50
• Zeffirelli's: Compston Road; 015394 33685; ££ (for price categories see p71)
• Rydal Mount: Rydal; 015394 33002; open Mar–Oct: 9:30am–5pm daily, Nov, Dec & Feb: 11am–4pm Wed–Sun; adm £6

Top 10 Features

1. Walk to Stock Ghyll Force
2. St Mary's Parish Church
3. Shopping
4. Jenkins Crag
5. Waterhead
6. Armitt Collection
7. Bridge House
8. Ambleside Climbing Wall
9. Zeffirelli's
10. Rydal Mount

1 Walk to Stock Ghyll Force

The leafy path up to Stock Ghyll Force *(above)* starts behind the Salutation Hotel. It is a short, steep walk to reach the lovely waterfall, where you can find a suitable rock and enjoy a picnic.

2 St Mary's Parish Church

This fine Gothic-Revival building is the work of Sir George Gilbert Scott. It features choir stalls carved with the images of saints and a 1940s mural depicting the town's Rushbearing Ceremony.

3 Shopping

Selling climbing gear, walking socks, books about the region, art works and picnic fare, Ambleside's cluster of attractive shops provides plenty of choices.

Jenkins Crag
This stony, rocky outcrop *(above)* provides a great view over Windermere, and is a good hike from Waterhead. You can walk to Townend *(see p11)* and Troutbeck.

Waterhead
A half-hour walk south of Ambleside, Waterhead sits on the shore of Windermere. There are no specific sights, but it is a pretty place where you can relax by the lake.

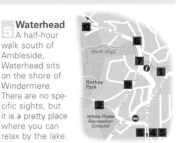

Armitt Collection
This excellent local history museum also houses collages by artist Kurt Schwitters (1887–1948), who came here to escape Nazi persecution.

Bridge House
This high-arched picturesque little building *(above)* straddles the Stock Beck river. Built as an apple store and once housing a family with six children, it is now home to a National Trust shop.

Ambleside Climbing Wall
An exciting venue at the heart of Ambleside. This five-storey building has a 10.5-m (35-ft) climbing wall and a bouldering room for developing skills. Café Altitude serves locally sourced food and overlooks the wall with glass viewing panels.

Zeffirelli's
A visit to Zef's is a must for any visitor to Ambleside. The rugged stone building houses a cinema and the restaurant here serves up excellent pizzas. Special deals combining dinner and cinema tickets are available. There is a café and jazz club upstairs.

Rydal Mount
Wordsworth and his family moved to Rydal Mount *(right)* in 1813, and he lived here until Mary's death in 1859. It was a much-loved family home and the original paintings, furniture, along with personal effects are still in situ.

Rushbearing Festival
This festival centres around the church of St Mary's and is held in early July. Children parade around the village with rush crosses, and then lay them on the floor of the church. The ancient ceremony dates back to the time when the church floor was made of compacted earth and covered with rushes (see p42).

🔟 The Langdale Valley

The Langdale Valley is the best area to see the beauty and grandeur of the Lake District. More accessible than Wasdale, the valley is nonetheless sculpted on a truly epic scale, with the steep, verdant fell walls giving way to even higher and sterner mountain ranges. This place is a hiker's heaven, and the attractive villages in the valley do their utmost to keep walkers fed and watered. Probably the nicest of these settlements is the riverside village of Elterwater.

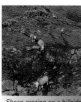

Sheep grazing on a hillside below Stickle Ghyll

✪ Do not underestimate the perils of driving over the passes here, and do not attempt them after dark.

🅾 Do stop by at one of Langdale's iconic pubs: Wainwrights Inn, the Britannia Inn or the Old Dungeon Ghyll Hotel.

• Map E5
• Hiker's Bar, Old Dungeon Ghyll Hotel: Old Dungeon Ghyll, Langdale; 015394 37272
• Touchstone Interiors: Skelwith Bridge; 015394 34002

Top 10 Features

1. Skelwith Bridge
2. Crinkle Crags
3. Cumbria Way
4. Elterwater
5. Wrynose Pass
6. Chapel Stile
7. Colwith Force
8. Stickle Ghyll
9. Blea Tarn
10. Hiker's Bar, Old Dungeon Ghyll Hotel

1 Skelwith Bridge
The tiny village of Skelwith Bridge *(above)* is focussed around the bridge that spans the Brathay. The settlement was a centre for the slate-mining industry and visitors can still buy articles made from the blue-green slate at Touchstone Interiors.

2 Crinkle Crags
The evocative name of Crinkle Crags derives from the five rises and dips of this line of fells. Part of two major mountain rings, these hills comprise one of Langdale Valley's classic routes and are praised by Wainwright *(see p41)* in his Pictorial Guides.

3 Cumbria Way
Running from Ulverston in the south to Carlisle in the north, the 120-km (75-mile) Cumbria Way *(left)* cuts a scenic swathe through the Langdale Valley. Visitors can stay at one of the Dungeon Ghyll hotels or the Stickleback Tavern.

4 Elterwater
This charming village has rugged stone cottages wreathed in honey-suckle and the River Brathay running through it *(left)*.

5 Wrynose Pass
Featuring narrow staggering inclines, Wrynose Pass will give nervous drivers palpitations. However, it rewards with dramatic and stark mountain views.

6 Chapel Stile
This pretty slate-quarrying village on the Brathay is home to a simple chapel *(below)*, and to one of the Lakes' classic watering holes: cosy Wainwrights Inn.

7 Colwith Force
Secluded Colwith Force tumbles down 12 m (40 ft) of mossy rocks edged by wood-land. It can be reached on a verdant footpath from Skelwith Bridge.

8 Stickle Ghyll
The cascades of the waterfall at Stickle Ghyll are dramatic, especially if there has been heavy rain. This forms the starting point for a steep, hour-long hike up to the 450-m (1,500-ft) high Stickle Tarn.

9 Blea Tarn
Tranquil Blea Tarn sits on the road between Little and Great Langdale, and is stocked with perch, pike and brown trout. Little Langdale Tarn is another nearby beauty spot. Call 015394 41197 for a day permit to fish.

10 Hiker's Bar, Old Dungeon Ghyll Hotel
Rugged furniture, local ales and hearty pub grub define this bar *(below)*, a popular venue for walkers. Book ahead for the hotel's restaurant.

Norse Names

First-time visitors to the Lakes are likely to be puzzled by the distinctive names bestowed on the region's ravines (ghylls), hills (fells), small mountain lakes (tarns), clearings (thwaites), streams (becks), peaks (pikes) waterfalls (forces), islands (holms) and valleys (dales). Many of these words derive from the language of the Norse people who arrived in the 9th century and, contrary to their violent image, settled here to farm.

🔟 Wordsworth's Lake District

William Wordsworth and the epic landscape of the Lake District are forever linked in the public imagination. Born in Cockermouth in 1770, Wordsworth died at Rydal Mount in 1850, and throughout the region there are umpteen sites associated with him. These range from pretty Dove Cottage, where he lived with his sister Dorothy and extended family, to isolated Easedale Tarn, immortalized in The Prelude. *Arm yourself with his* Selected Poems *and Dorothy's journals, to get a real feel of the places and peaks he adored.*

House of Wordsworth's grandparents

⭐ **Dove Cottage** is a popular attraction. Try going early or late in the day to avoid the crowds.

☕ **The Tearoom at Rydal Mount** is a lovely spot with outdoor seating.

• *Wordsworth House: Crown Street, Cockermouth; Map C2; 01900 824805; open mid-Mar–Oct: 11am–4pm Sat–Wed; adm £6.20* • *Rydal Mount: Rydal; Map F5; 015394 33002; open Mar–Oct: 9:30am–5pm daily, Nov, Dec & Feb: 11am–4pm Wed–Sun; adm £6.75* • *Dove Cottage: SE of Grasmere; Map E5; 015394 35544; open 9:30am–5pm (4pm in winter); adm £7.50* • *Hawkshead School: Hawkshead; Map M2; open Apr–Sept: 10am–1pm & 2–5pm Mon–Sat, 1–5pm Sun, Oct: 10am–1pm & 2–3:30pm Mon–Sat, Sun 1–3:30pm; adm £2.50*

Top 10 Features

1. Dora's Field
2. Rydal Mount
3. Wordsworth House, Cockermouth
4. St Oswald's, Grasmere
5. Dove Cottage
6. Greenhead Ghyll
7. Easedale Tarn Walk
8. Penrith
9. Hawkshead School
10. All Saints Church, Cockermouth

Dora's Field
1 Heartbroken by their daughter Dora's death at the age of 43, Wordsworth and his wife planted daffodils in her memory beneath Rydal Mount *(above)*. The flowers are at their best in March.

Rydal Mount
2 This relatively grand house was Wordsworth's home in his later years. You can see the poet's books, paintings, the immortal couch on which he lay *(main image)*, and his summer house in the garden.

Wordsworth House, Cockermouth
3 Late 18th-century life is brilliantly re-created at Wordsworth's birthplace. Visiting kids can try on clothes, play with toys and even help out with chores.

St Oswald's, Grasmere
4 Located in central Grasmere, the grave-yard of St Oswald's *(left)* shelters the tombs of Wordsworth, his wife Mary, three of their children who died tragically young, his sister Dorothy, and other members of his extended family.

Dove Cottage
Built in the 17th-century, Dove Cottage *(right)* provides an insight into the social history of the Lakes and the spartan lives of the Wordsworths.

Greenhead Ghyll
The rushing mountain stream of Greenhead Ghyll features in Wordsworth's tragic pastoral poem "Michael". It is reached via an attractive path just east of Grasmere.

Easedale Tarn Walk
Wordsworth's favourite hike *(below)* leads northwest out of Grasmere on a lovely leafy path, and then climbs steeply up a stony rugged path to reach the beautiful tarn (mountain lake). Allow three hours to get up and back.

Penrith
Home to Wordsworth's mother, Penrith was where he and his wife went to infant school. Visitors can make a trip here to see his grandparents' house.

Hawkshead School
The busy village of Hawkshead is home to the rugged little grammar school that the poet attended. You can still see the signature that he scored into his wooden desk *(left)*.

All Saints Church, Cockermouth
Wordsworth's father died when he was 13, and is buried in the mid-19th-century All Saints Church *(right)*, constructed in the early English style. It also has a memorial window to Wordsworth designed by John Hardman.

Wordsworth's Guide to the Lakes

It is the irony of many a guidebook that the writer resents tourists trammelling the area they love. Yet, in writing, they only serve to entice more visitors to the place. Such was the case with Wordsworth's *Guide to the Lakes*, first published in 1810. His preoccupations with the impact of tourists in this region still have relevance. But his writing described the the Lakes in such a marvellous way that people were inevitably lured in vast numbers.

Left **Books for sale, Dove Cottage shop** Centre **Daffodils, Ullswater** Right **Esthwaite Water**

Literary Sites

Hill Top
Beatrix Potter's farmhouse is located 3 km (2 miles) from Windermere's western shore and is accessible via a little car ferry.

The Fish Hotel sign

Though coach trips have watered down the rural isolation, Hill Top still gives a real sense of Potter's life and craft *(see p10)*.

Esthwaite Water
Lying to the west of Hill Top, Esthwaite Water is stocked with trout and ringed by waterlilies. The lake was an inspiration for Beatrix Potter's *The Tale of Mr Jeremy Fisher*, the story of a waistcoat-wearing frog. Map M2

Keswick
This was home to another literary giant associated with the Lakes – Samuel Taylor Coleridge.

Keswick, with mountains in the background

His fearless walks up peaks such as Scafell were influential in establishing mountaineering as a popular activity *(see pp28–9)*.

The Fish Hotel, Buttermere
Although mainly known as a broadcaster, Melvyn Bragg is also a novelist. His best known work is the historical novel *The Maid of Buttermere*, based on the real-life story of Mary Robinson, the daughter of the Fish Hotel landlord who was seduced by a bigamist. Map C4

Nibthwaite
A village at the southern end of Coniston Water, Nibthwaite inspired Arthur Ransome *(see p41)* to write his *Swallows and Amazons* series. Map M3

Haystacks
Located south of Buttermere, Haystacks was Alfred Wainwright's favourite hike – he even chose to have his ashes scattered here. He wrote of the mountain that it, "stands unabashed and unashamed in the midst of a circle of much loftier fells, like a shaggy terrier in the company of foxhounds." Map D4

Ullswater
If you time your trip to the Lakes to see "a host of golden daffodils" on the Ullswater shore *(see pp82–7)*, spare a thought for

William Wordsworth

Wordsworth's poetic career was marked by his meeting with Samuel Taylor Coleridge, which resulted in the publication of the Lyrical Ballads, *a landmark in Romantic poetry, interwoven with the ideals of the French Revolution. The other great influence in his work was the sublime landscape of the Lakes. Wordsworth moved here with his sister Dorothy in 1799, and immersed himself in his natural surroundings. Dorothy's close observations, recorded in her journals, were an inspiration for William. His contemporaries felt he had abandoned his radicalism and written his best work by the time he became Poet Laureate (1843–1850). The Prelude, the philosophical and spiritual autobiography he began in his late 20s, is considered his greatest work.*

Interior, Hawkshead Grammar School

The Wordsworth Trust

This trust operating Dove Cottage aims to make it more than just a memorial to the great man. They have a poet in residence and organize workshops throughout the year.

Wordsworth's sister Dorothy. Her beautiful diary entry about the flowers inspired one of the most famous poems in the English language – *Daffodils*.

Dove Cottage

8 Following the tenancy of the Wordsworths, Dove Cottage was occupied by the writer and intellectual Thomas de Quincey *(see p41)* who lived here for ten years. However, de Quincey's alterations to the property, and his marriage to a farmer's daughter, caused a rift with his former idol Wordsworth *(see p9)*.

Brantwood

9 Home to John Ruskin from 1872 until his death in 1900, Brantwood has a wonderful location above Coniston Water. Ruskin wrote widely on social justice and the arts in general *(see p24)*.

Ambleside

10 Harriet Martineau, said to be the first female journalist in England, was also renowned as a feminist, abolitionist and philosopher. She spent the latter part of her life in Ambleside *(see pp16–17)* in a house named The Knoll.

10 Coniston Water

Coniston tends to get rather overlooked, with many visitors making a beeline for larger Windermere. However, Coniston's long, slender stretch of water is all the better for being less visited, and has lovely attractions such as Ruskin's beautiful home, Brantwood, as well as some wonderful walks. Visitors can explore the lake on various craft, including the National Trust's 19th-century gondola.

Exhibit on display at the Ruskin Museum

Flowers in bloom at Brantwood

🌸 Come in the summer season for a trip on the National Trust gondola.

🍽 Head for Jumping Jenny's restaurant at Brantwood, which has a lovely terrace with lake views.

• Map M2
• Brantwood: Coniston; 015394 41396; open Mar–Nov: 10:30am–5:30pm, daily; Nov–Mar: 10:30am–4:30pm daily; adm £6.30; www.brantwood.org.uk
• Steam Yacht Gondola: 015394 41533; runs Apr–Oct; adm £9.90; www.nationaltrust.org.uk
• Ruskin Museum: Coniston; 015394 32733 open Mar–mid-Nov: 10am–5:30pm (to 3:30pm in winter); adm £5.25; www.ruskinmuseum.com
• Dodgson Wood Campsite; 01229 885663

Top 10 Features

1. Brantwood
2. The Old Man of Coniston
3. Grizedale Forest
4. Coniston Village
5. Tarn Hows
6. Peel Island
7. Steam Yacht Gondola
8. Dodgson Wood
9. Boat Hire
10. Ruskin Museum

1 Brantwood
The lovely interiors at Brantwood *(above)* feature John Ruskin's collection of art and furniture. The gardens have a zigzag path imitating Dante's journey to paradise, an ancient woodland and a fern garden.

2 The Old Man of Coniston
It takes a couple of hours to hike from Coniston village to the Old Man of Coniston, a 800 m (2,634 ft) fell with views to the coast and the Scafell Massif.

3 Grizedale Forest
This swathe of pine, oak and spruce forest *(left)* features over 60 sculptures to explore along the paths. It is also home to Go Ape tree top adventures and single track mountain bike trails.

4 Coniston Village
The copper-mining village of Coniston *(above)* is a compact and engaging little place, with a couple of great pubs, a museum and decent accommodation.

5 Tarn Hows
Bequeathed to the National Trust by Beatrix Potter, Tarn Hows *(main image)* is one of the most famous beauty spots in the region.

6 Peel Island
Immortalised as Wild Cat Island in the *Swallows and Amazons* series *(see p41)*, this tiny, wooded island sits on the southern end of the lake.

7 Steam Yacht Gondola
The National Trust rebuilt this elegant Victorian steam boat *(left)* that had sunk in a storm and spent much of the 1960s at the bottom of the lake. It ferries passengers up the lake to Brantwood.

8 Dodgson Wood
This ancient woodland *(right)*, a Site of Special Scientific Interest, has a camp site perfect for watersports and activities in Grizedale Forest.

9 Boat Hire
Head to the lake shore near Coniston village to rent all sorts of craft, including electric boats and kayaks.

Donald Campbell and Bluebird

Car and motorboat racer Donald Campbell died in an accident in Coniston in 1967 while he was trying to break the world water-speed record. The boat he was racing, *Bluebird*, was recovered from the lake in 2001 and lovingly restored. It may take to Coniston Water again as there is a plan to suspend the ban on motor boats in *Bluebird's* honour.

10 Ruskin Museum
This gem of a local history museum *(right)* has a collection dedicated to artist and critic, John Ruskin. Established in 1901, the museum also has a section on racer Donald Campbell, as well as exhibits on local industries such as mining and lace-making.

The Lake District's Top 10

9

TOP 10 Wasdale

This valley is simply one of the wildest and most impressive places in Britain. From the village of Gosforth, a narrow road leads past lonely West Water and ends at the valley head with England's mightiest mountains – Scafell, Scafell Pike and Great Gable – rising before you. Drop in for a pint at the venerable Wasdale Head Inn, pitch your tent at either of the camp sites, stock up at the outdoor shops, or simply enjoy some quiet time at the tiny late-Victorian church. Wasdale offers all this, and the best mountain views you will ever see.

Road sign for Wasdale

🌀 **Wasdale is as wild as it looks. Do not think about walking here without adequate gear, supplies and an Ordnance Survey map. Tell someone where you are planning to go before you head off.**

🍴 **The Wasdale Head Inn is by far the best choice for a meal. Do try the Herdwick lamb and mutton.**

• Map D5
• Wasdale Head Inn: Wasdale Head, near Gosforth; 019467 26229; ££ (for price categories see p117)

Top 10 Features

1 Wasdale Head
2 Canoeing, West Water
3 Mountain Biking
4 Santon Bridge
5 Wasdale Head Inn
6 Viking Cross, Gosforth
7 St Olaf's Church
8 Scafell
9 Napes Needle
10 Great Gable

1 Wasdale Head
Quite literally the end of the road – the country lane peters out into the tiny hamlet of Wasdale Head *(below)*, which offers a spectacular view of a ring of soaring mountain peaks.

3 Mountain Biking
Little-travelled country roads and a network of rugged paths make Wasdale a great challenge for fit and experienced mountain bikers.

2 Canoeing, West Water
Only 15 people are allowed to canoe at one time on West Water, meaning that this stretch of chilly water, backed by imposing scree-covered hillsides, feels all the more remote.

4 Santon Bridge
This is a quiet and unobtrusive Lake District village *(below)* by the side of the River Irt. There is a great pub here – the Bridge Inn – which hosts the idiosyncratic "World's Biggest Liar" competition every year.

Wasdale Head Inn

A venerable and handsome place, which is almost the only option here other than camping. For hearty meals, real ales and hiking tales, make for cosy Ritson's Bar *(left)* round the side of the Inn.

Viking Cross, Gosforth

This slender 2-m (14-ft) high Viking Cross in the graveyard of St Mary's in Gosforth *(main image)* was carved in around AD 940. It features intricate knot-work and imagery which combines a Christian theme with Nordic figures.

St Olaf's Church

Supposedly the smallest church in the country, St Olaf's *(below)* was rebuilt in the late 19th century, though there has been a church on the site since medieval times.

Scafell

As the highest peak in England, Scafell is no pushover. Keep an eye on the weather and make sure you are well kitted out *(see p112)*. This peak is an enjoyable challenge and the reward is a superb view.

Napes Needle

For most people, just looking at the rocky pinnacle of Napes Needle is enough of an adrenalin boost. The ascent is only recommended for experienced climbers as it presents a tremendous test.

Lying in the Lakes

The tradition of tall tales was supposedly created in Wasdale in the 19th century by publican Will Ritson. He specialized in fantastical tales – Wordsworth is said to have been one of his listeners, along with many a gullible tourist. This tradition continues with the World's Biggest Liar competition *(see p43)*, a stand-up for fibbers, held at Bridge Inn *(see p103)*.

Great Gable

Pyramidal Great Gable *(above)* makes for a popular hike – it is accessible both from Wasdale and Seatoller *(see p94)*. A high pass called Windy Gap connects Great Gable to the smaller Green Gable.

🏵10 Keswick

A popular and busy little town, Keswick has plenty of attractions, although it is not quite as enticing as other lush Lakeland settlements. Its proximity to lovely Derwent Water however, makes the town a good base for walkers and nature enthusiasts. Keswick is also a handy option for rainy days, with museums, a market, a good repertory theatre and the beautiful and historic Alhambra Cinema.

Keswick Museum and Art Gallery

🌀 The Keswick Launch is a perfect way to tour the lake.

💬 The veggie café Lakeland Pedlar on Bell Close, is one of the most popular lunch stops in town.

• Cumberland Pencil Museum: Southey Works, Keswick; Map S4; 017687 73626; 9:30–4pm daily; adm £4; www.pencilmuseum. co.uk • Keswick Museum and Art Gallery (closed until Nov 2013): Fitz Park, Station Road; Map U4; 017687 73263; open 10am–4pm Tue–Sat • Alhambra Cinema: St John St; Map T5; 017687 72195; adm £5.50; www.keswick-alhambra. co.uk • Moot Hall: Keswick Market Square; Map T5; 017687 72645 • Puzzling Place: Museum Square; Map T5; 017687 775102; open 11am–5:30pm daily (10:30am–5pm school hols); adm £3.75; www. puzzlingplace.co.uk • Theatre by the Lake: Map S6; 017687 74411; www.theatrebythelake. co.uk

Top 10 Features

1. Puzzling Place
2. Derwent Water
3. Theatre by the Lake
4. Alhambra Cinema
5. Crosthwaite
6. Cumberland Pencil Museum
7. Keswick Museum and Art Gallery
8. Castlerigg Stone Circle
9. Keswick Market
10. Moot Hall

Puzzling Place

A fascinating and fun excursion into the wonderful world of optical illusions *(left)*. There are plenty of things to challenge your brain in this mind-bogglingly curious place – from the anti-gravity room to the hologram gallery by way of interactive exhibits, artworks and sculptures.

Derwent Water

Circled by lofty fells, Derwent Water *(below)* is dotted with wooded islands that were settled by early Christians in the 7th century. Seven landing stages around the lake provide regular stop-offs for the Keswick Launch.

Theatre by the Lake

This beautifully sited theatre has a six-month summer repertory season plus other shows through the year. The theatre exhibits art and is also a great place for a drink.

Check www.keswick-launch.co.uk for lake cruise timetables.

4 Alhambra Cinema

A glamorous 1913 cinema *(left)* showing a mixture of art-house and popular films. The beautifully restored little auditorium is done up in red velvet and white stucco.

5 Crosthwaite

Take a stroll to the west of town to see the ancient church at Crosthwaite, with its languorous marble effigy *(main image)* of the poet Robert Southey who is buried in the churchyard.

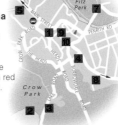

6 Cumberland Pencil Museum

This lively local-history museum *(above)* charts the history of graphite mining in the region since the medieval period and pencil production in the 19th century.

7 Keswick Museum and Art Gallery

Housed in a Victorian-Gothic building, this museum opened in 1898. It remains unmodernized, except for the arrival of electricity. Exhibits include a set of musical stones, a penny farthing and manuscripts by Wordsworth, Coleridge and Ruskin.

8 Castlerigg Stone Circle

Erected around 3000 BC, this spacious circle of 38 stones *(right)* enjoys a wonderful setting, with the light on the surrounding fells providing an ever-shifting backdrop.

9 Keswick Market

Market days are Thursdays and Saturdays. All around the Moot Hall there are stalls *(left)* selling a range of local produce including food, crafts and clothes.

10 Moot Hall

Built in 1813, the Moot Hall *(right)* is an imposing structure right in the busy town centre. Earlier used as the town hall and prison, today it houses the tourist information centre and various temporary exhibitions. Look out for the one-handed clock.

Keswick Festivals

The array of festivals in Keswick reflect the vibrancy of this little town. There is the Keswick Film Festival in February, branded the "friendly film festival"; the literary event "Words by the Water" in March; a well-regarded international Jazz Festival in May; and a Beer Festival in June. All this plus the usual round of summer agricultural fairs: these generally feature an abundance of animals and are great for kids.

Left **Depiction of a Border Reivers Cattle Raid** Right **Neolithic Stone Circle at Castlerigg**

 Moments in History

3000 BC: Neolithic People
The first farmers in the Lakes area also created the atmospheric stone circle at Castlerigg *(see p29)*. Stone axes found at Scafell and bronze tools at Ambleside shed some light on the lives of these early inhabitants.

Roman Hilltop Fort, Hardknott Pass

AD 69: The Romans
The significant Roman presence in the Lakes, associated with Hadrian's Wall, built to mark the northern limits of the British Roman Empire, is still tangible. The most impressive remnant is the lonely hilltop fort on the Hardknott Pass, which gives some indication of the formidable military power of the invaders.

AD 800–900: The Vikings
The Vikings arrived with less of a vengeance in the Lakes than they did in the other areas. In fact, the Norse invaders were part of a wider wave of settlement, rather than arriving here bent on rape and pillage. They are remembered in many of the poetic local place names and terms.

The Medieval Period: Lakeland Industries
The medieval period saw the establishment of sheep-farming, as well as the beginning of a long tradition of mining. Graphite was extracted for pencil-making and glazing. Slate and copper mining also developed and gradually became integral to the local economy.

1400–1700: Border Raids
The Border Reivers threatened the area in the 15th–16th century, launching raids from the border between Scotland and England, rustling livestock, kidnapping and extorting money. The distinctive "pele" towers were built as defences during this period. Many of these still stand and have formed the basis for later country houses.

The Eighteenth Century: The Romantic Period
Wordsworth, Coleridge, Turner, Gainsborough, and Constable were the poets and artists who immortalized the Lake District, deeply inspired by the folklore and the landscape. They were also the reluctant inspiration of the Lakes' tourism industry.

William Wordsworth

Preceding pages **Derwent Water, Keswick**

Steam Railway in the Lakes

7 1847: The Railways

The first passenger railway line between Kendal and Windermere was completed in 1847, and transformed the latter into a boom town. It also brought large numbers of tourists and walkers, cementing the popularity of the Lakes.

8 1895 and 1951: Conservation

These dates mark milestones in protecting the area from over-development. In 1895 the National Trust was founded; its land ownership in the area owes much to Beatrix Potter, who made large bequests to the Trust. The Lake District National Park was established in 1951 to prevent insensitive development.

9 2001: Farming Crisis

The Foot and Mouth crisis of 2001 was a serious blow to the farmers in the Lakes – many had to destroy their livestock. Tourists were banned, and so farm B&Bs also suffered. The recent move towards using local produce is now a source of optimism for the region's hill farmers.

10 2009: Flooding

In November 2009 the Lakes were hit by the most severe floods in a whole millenium. The western areas, especially Cockermouth, were the worst affected. Bridges were swept away and the army was brought in to help during the emergency.

Top 10 Prehistoric and Roman Sites

1 Long Meg and Her Daughters
A perfect circle of 69 stones, dating from 1500 BC. ◊ *Little Salkeld, the Eden Valley* • *Map H2*

2 Mayburgh Henge
This circular earthwork has a single standing stone at the centre. ◊ *3 km (2 miles) south of Penrith* • *Map G2*

3 Ravenglass Roman Bath House
The 4-m (13-ft) high walls suggest the scale of this Roman bath house, built in AD 130. ◊ *Ravenglass* • *Map J2*

4 Castlerigg Stone Circle
Dating back to 3000 BC, this is among the most atmospheric sites in Britain. ◊ *Near Keswick* • *Map E3*

5 Hardknott Roman Fort
A lonely road takes you to this imposing Roman fort. ◊ *Hardknott Pass* • *Map D6*

6 Ambleside Roman Fort
There is little left of this fort, but it is a lovely verdant spot. ◊ *Ambleside* • *Map F5*

7 Blakeley Rise Stone Circle
This lovely moorland site has 11 low stones. ◊ *South of Ennerdale Bridge* • *Map B4*

8 Swinside Stone Circle
Impressive Swinside has a circle of 55 stones in a lush farmland. ◊ *Near Broughton-in-Furness* • *Map L3*

9 The Langdale Boulders
This cluster of craggy, patterned rocks is a remarkable example of prehistoric art. ◊ *Near Chapel Stile* • *Map E5*

10 Rock Art, Ullswater
See rocks scored with lines and patterns dating back 5,000 years. ◊ *Map F4*

Left **Laurel and Hardy Museum** Centre **The Beacon** Right **Interior, Ruskin Museum**

TOP 10 Museums and Galleries

1 Keswick Museum and Art Gallery

This museum is a step-back-in-time experience, with a fascinating Victorian collection of curiosities and treasures housed in old glass cases, as well as letters and memorabilia associated with Wordsworth and other Lakes' poets and writers *(see p28)*.

Keswick Museum and Art Gallery

2 Castlegate House Gallery

An interesting contemporary commercial space in Cockermouth, which focuses on the work of 20th-century British artists. The works of emerging artists are showcased, as are pieces by iconic names such as Winifred Nicholson and LS Lowry. On display are paintings, sculptures, ceramics and prints. ◈ *Castlegate House, Cockermouth*
• Map C2 • 01900 822149 • Open 10:30am–5pm Mon, Fri & Sat • www. castlegatehouse.co.uk

3 Ruskin Museum

A celebration of all things Ruskin-related. The museum examines his life as a still-influential art critic and historian and exhibits his attractive watercolours and drawings. Local industries are also explored, and there are displays of delicate linen and lace. ◈ *Coniston • Map M2 • 015394 32733 • Open mid-Mar to mid-Nov 10am–5:30pm daily • Adm*
• www.ruskinmuseum.com

4 Laurel and Hardy Museum

An engaging though slightly timeworn collection of memorabilia celebrating the Ulverston origins of comic star Stan Laurel: the museum plays Stan and Ollie's slapstick movies on a loop. A statue in Country Square in the town com-memorates the duo. ◈ *Brogden Street, Ulverston • Map M4 • 01229 582292 • Open Feb–Dec 10am–5pm daily • Adm • www.laurel-and-hardy.co.uk*

5 Windermere Steamboat Museum

Dedicated to the craft that ply the Lakes, this lakeside museum's collection includes Dolly, a mid-19th-century steam launch raised from Ullswater, where she had languished for an incredible 65 years, and Margaret, the oldest yacht in the UK, built in Whitehaven in 1780 *(see p10)*.

Sculpture at Castlegate House Gallery

6 The Wordsworth Museum and Art Gallery

Wordsworth's life and times are examined in absorbing detail, through letters, taped readings of his poems, portraiture and reminiscences. There is an emphasis on the rural life explored in the poet's poetry and entertaining detail on his domestic sphere – you can see his toothscrapers, lunch box and panama hat, as well as Dorothy's tiny shoes *(see p8)*.

The Wordsworth Museum and Art Gallery

7 Abbot Hall Art Gallery

The elegant restored Georgian interiors showcase a series of portraits of Lady Anne Clifford, commissioned in the mid-17th-century to mark her acquisition of her legacy after a 40-year battle. The gallery also has an excellent collection of Romney portraits, and changing contemporary fine-art shows upstairs *(see p12)*. ✎ *www. abbothall.org.uk*

8 The Beacon

An imaginative, interactive museum housed in a lighthouse-like building on the harbour, The Beacon explores Copeland's turbulent and fascinating story. There's rich background on the slave trade and smuggling, as well as temporary photography exhibitions to bring things up to date.

✎ *West Strand, Whitehaven • Map A4 • 01946 592302 • Open 10am–4:30pm Tue–Sun • Adm • www. thebeacon-whitehaven.co.uk*

9 The Armitt Collection

The Armitt Collection comprises both local-history exhibits and contemporary art. There are displays dedicated to German exile Kurt Schwitters *(see p40)*, and some Beatrix Potter *(see p66)* treasures: in 1943 Potter gave the gallery 450 of her watercolours depicting funghi, fish and mosses *(see p16)*.

✎ *www.thearmittcollection.com*

10 Museum of Lakeland Life and Industry

This award-winning museum takes you back through time to explore the history of the Lake District and its inhabitants through interactive displays and recreated rooms from significant periods in Lakeland life. There are also displays devoted to Arthur Ransome and to the Arts & Crafts movement, which flourished in the Lakes *(see p12)*.

✎ *www.lakelandmuseum.org.uk*

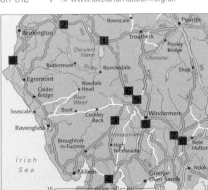

Left **Cushions at Yew Tree Barn** Centre **Low Sizergh Barn** Right **Lemon and Lime Relish**

🔟 Places to Shop

1 Kentmere Pottery
A long-established pottery based alongside a 13th-century mill, Kentmere Pottery stocks handmade ceramics, bowls, boxes, lamps and mugs. ✎ *Kentmere, near Kendal • Map P1 • 01539 821621*

Kentmere Pottery

Visitors can meet the artists and also drop by the Hat Trick Café, lined with old photographs and prints and serving traditional lemonade, tea and cakes. ✎ *Low Newton near Grange-over-Sands • Map N4 • 015395 31498*

2 Low Sizergh Barn
The wonderful timbered barn building with its weathered beams is home to an excellent farm shop, selling their own produce plus the best of Lakeland meats, preserves and baked goods. They also sell a range of clothes, local pottery, carpets, gardening equipment and handmade soaps. ✎ *Sizergh • Map P3 • 015395 60426*

3 The Gallery, Yew Tree Barn
A Victorian barn housing a cornucopia of gifts, from Lakeland furniture to hand-made ceramics to bold jewellery.

4 Hawkshead Relish Company
This family-run company in picturesque Hawkshead makes the very best of fine local ingredients to produce pickles, chutneys, preserves, relishes, jams and – their best seller – red onion marmalade *(see p69)*.

5 Sarah Nelson's Gingerbread Shop
Gingerbread is made to a secret recipe in this tiny whitewashed building beside Grasmere church. The pretty blue and white packaging of the biscuits make this a good gift. You can also buy traditional rum butter here *(see p8)*.

6 Keswick Brewing Company
High-quality cask and bottled ales are created by combining traditional and modern ingredients at this historic craft brewery. Visitors can take a tour of the brewery and peruse the bottles of bitters and pale ales. The brewery even does a seasonal range of ales, including a malty Christmas ale that makes a good alternative festive gift *(see p95)*.

The Gallery, Yew Tree Barn

7 Pooley Bridge Market
This monthly farmers' market offers fresh fish, award-winning sausages, fresh baked goods and cheeses. A great place to stock your picnic basket before heading to Ullswater Lake.
⊗ *The Sun Inn, Pooley Bridge • Map G3 • 017684 86205 • Open Apr–Sep: 10am–2:30pm last Sun of the month*

8 Honister Slate Mine Shop
Take the rugged road to Honister and follow up a tour of the slate mine with a visit to the onsite shop. You will find a range of products fashioned out of slate, from coffee tables to clocks and placemats. You can also order personalized house signs *(see p95)*.

The Bookshop at The Tinner's Rabbit

9 The Bookshop at The Tinner's Rabbit
This award-winning bookshop has an eclectic collection of local books, maps, and pottery.
⊗ *48 Market Street, Ulverston • Map M4 • 01229 588858*

10 Castlegate House Gallery
As the name suggests, the experience of visiting this gallery is of visiting someone's home: a beautiful, light-filled Georgian home. The walls are hung with art – there is a specialism in northern English and Scottish artists – and the spacious garden is dotted with sculptures *(see p95)* .

Top 10 Things to Buy

1 Pottery
Locally made pottery is a Lake District speciality, and makes a fine gift or souvenir.

2 Paintings and Drawings
Independent galleries sell beautiful artworks depicting the fells and lakes.

3 Photographs
Epic landscapes and changing light make the Lakes really photogenic; many galleries stock photographic prints.

4 Farm Foods
Jam, relish, cheese, bread and cake: the delicious local produce in the Lakes is a must-buy.

5 Beer
Microbreweries abound in this region, offering a wealth of delicious and quirkily named ales.

6 Slate
Handpainted signs, birdbaths and sundials in dark grey slate are some typical Lakeland souvenirs.

7 Books and Maps
Fiction, fauna, history, walks, and topography – the local bookshops have it all.

8 Ice Cream
Imaginative flavours and local organic ingredients make Lakeland ice cream a treat worth buying in bulk.

9 Crystal
Watch crystal being made at the Lakes Glass Centre in Ulverston and then buy some.
⊗ *Oubas Hill, Ulverston • Map M4 • 01229 581385*

10 Damson Gin
Damson plums are distilled into a delicious ruby-red liqueur after soaking in a gin and sugar syrup. ⊗ *Map F4*

Left **Michelin starred food at L'Enclume** Centre **Gilpin Lodge** Right **The Brown Horse Inn**

Restaurants

1 Lucy's On a Plate

An Ambleside institution, Lucy's is a snug, bistro-like place that specializes in hearty, locally sourced food such as Cumbrian lamb and Grizedale venison. Puddings, including sticky toffee, are especially good.

A delicious dessert at Lucy's

The convivial atmosphere means it is fun in a group, as well as for a relaxing breakfast with a weekend newspaper *(see p81)*.

2 Quince & Medlar, Cockermouth

A historic Georgian building with lovely wood-panelling and lit by candles, Quince and Medlar features excellent vegetarian food. The restaurant only uses seasonal ingredients to create dishes such as spinach cream cheese and Wensleydale gateau or smoked Cumberland cheese and mushroom roulade *(see p97)*.

3 Jumble Room

This lively little restaurant brings a dash of style and colour to Grasmere. Blues and jazz

The cosy interior of Jumble Room

music drifts through the restaurant. The menu is international but they are also famous for their fish and hand-cut chips, served with mushy peas *(see p81)*.

4 Rustique, Ulverston

A great little deli and restaurant with freshly cooked and mostly local food. Rustique has an à la carte option, and the main menu offers dishes such as roast beef fillet and chicken with black pudding mousse *(see p71)*.

5 Drunken Duck

This terrific inn just north of Hawkshead has a warm, informal ambience. Their restaurant boasts excellent and imaginative food, with a strong emphasis on meat and game. Enjoy home-brewed ales along with specialities such as smoked haddock and pan-fried monkfish with sautéed baby leeks. The bread and butter pudding is a must-try *(see p71)*.

6 The Brown Horse Inn, Winster

A fine roadside inn, The Brown Horse serves up exceptional pub food and traditional fare with ingredients sourced from their own farm or within a 5-km (3-mile) radius. Try their delicious rack of spring Cumbrian lamb or loin of Winster venison. Good ales and wines accompany the food *(see p71)*.

7 Holbeck Ghyll Country House Hotel, Windermere

This family-run country house has perhaps the best restaurant in the region. The food is Michelin-starred – try the seven-course taster menu or indulge in the excellent mains such as guinea fowl, sea bass or veal *(see p71)*.

8 Miller Howe

Located in the luxurious Windermere hotel with fantastic views of the lake, Miller Howe offers elegant main courses such as Cumbrian beef fillet, Holker Hall venison and lamb saddle. There is also an extensive vegetarian menu, a value-for-money Sunday lunch and great desserts *(see p71)*.

The dining room at Miller Howe

9 L'Enclume, Cartmel

A marvellous Michelin-starred restaurant in the southern Lakes, L'Enclume uses local wild produce. Located in a former village smithy, this restaurant serves food that is innovative and masterfully presented, with a fresh and light taste provided by herbs, roots and even flowers *(see p71)*.

10 Gilpin Lodge, Windermere

The dining room at this rural retreat serves superb food. Try the roasted loin of Grizedale venison wrapped in smoked bacon, with spiced red cabbage, pickled damsons and chocolate sauce *(see p71)*.

Top 10 Culinary Specialities

1 Grasmere Gingerbread
Grasmere's special gingerbread is made to a secret recipe and enticingly wrapped in traditional packaging.

2 Sticky Toffee Pudding
Taste this irresistibly sweet confection in its birthplace, Cartmel.

3 Herdwick Lamb and Mutton
Do try the locally sourced lamb and mutton: a mainstay of menus in the Lakes.

4 Lakes Ice Cream
There are a few excellent outlets for home-made ice cream. Possibly the best is available at Syke farm. Map C4 • Buttermere

5 Kendal Mint Cake
Dense and tooth-meltingly sweet, Kendal Mint Cake is used by walkers as an instant energy-booster *(see p13)*.

6 Kendal Cheeses
Low Sizergh Barn *(see p36)* is a good place to source local farmhouse cheeses.

7 Cumberland Sausage
These tasty pork sausages are served coiled on the plate.

8 Morecambe Bay Potted Shrimps
Local shrimps are boiled in butter with spices, then sealed with butter and packed into pots.

9 Hawkshead Relish
Handmade in the village where Wordsworth went to school *(see p21)*, these relishes have no additives: red onion marmalade is the best seller.

10 Damson Gin and Jam
Damson gin and jam, from fruit picked in the Lyth Valley, make great souvenirs.

Left **Book by Arthur Ransome** Centre **Dove Cottage** Right **Works by Wordsworth**

Writers and Artists

1 Coleridge
Coleridge, along with Wordsworth, was a founder of the English Romantic movement. The Romanticism of these poets was inseparable from the transcendent beauty of the Lakes. Coleridge immersed himself in the landscape, taking long and daring hikes, which ultimately helped to establish climbing as a leisure pursuit.

2 William Wordsworth
Wordsworth's evocations of the Lake District's monumental splendour firmly placed the area on the tourist map, and continue to draw visitors today. The *Selected Poems* are a good introduction to his writing, and visits to Dove Cottage and Rydal Mount tell you much about the man himself *(see also pp20–21)*.

3 Dorothy Wordsworth
Much has been written about Dorothy's closeness to her brother William, focusing on her strained and strange account of his wedding to Mary. The truth of their relationship is unknown, but Dorothy's own observations of nature and of a vanished rural way of life are a must-read for a Lakes' visit.

4 George Romney
Born in Dalton-in-Furness in 1734, George Romney trained as a painter in Kendal before setting

Death of General Wolfe by George Romney

up as a society artist in London; he painted many portraits of Emma Hamilton, Nelson's lover. Fans of Romney's fluid and sensual portraits should make a beeline for the Abbot Hall Art Gallery in Kendal *(see p13)*.

5 Kurt Schwitters
Born in Hanover in 1887, Kurt Schwitters made the Lakes his home after he was branded a degenerate artist by the Nazis. He is known for his collages made from discarded materials and called *Merz Pictures*, examples of which can be seen at the Armitt Collection in Ambleside *(see p17)*.

Peter Rabbit

6 Beatrix Potter
Peter Rabbit and Jeremy Fisher need no introduction. Their creator Beatrix Potter's independence was hard-won as her parents were unsympathetic to her literary ambitions. Eventually, Potter's success enabled her to buy her home at Hill Top *(see p10)*.

7 Arthur Ransome

Arthur Ransome authored the perennial favourite, *Swallows and Amazons*, tales of childhood derring-do that were inspired by his holidays in Coniston. Ransome was also a journalist and foreign correspondent with a strong interest in Russia; his second wife was Trotsky's secretary.

8 Thomas de Quincey

The guides at Dove Cottage *(see p9)* make valiant efforts to tell the story of the building's second-most famous inhabitant, Thomas de Quincey. The author of *Confessions of an English Opium Eater* was drawn to the region by his adoration of Wordsworth, and lived in Dove Cottage for 10 years after the Wordsworths moved on.

Alfred Wainwright at work

9 Alfred Wainwright

Walker, author and alleged curmudgeon, Wainwright is an inescapable presence in the Lake District, even 20 years after his death. His monument is the 7-volume illustrated guides that still serve as great handbooks to local fell walks.

10 J M W Turner

The changing light on the mountains of the Lake District was a perfect subject for Turner, who visited the region in the late-18th century. His image of stormy Buttermere can be seen at the Tate Britain gallery in London.

Top 10 Books Set in the Lakes

1 The Lake District Series, Martin Edwards
Dark crime thrillers set in the Lakes.

2 Haweswater, Sarah Hall
A poetic family drama charting the demise of a farming community in the 1930s.

3 All Quiet on the Orient Express, Magnus Mills
A sinister yet comic tale of a bemused Lakes' visitor trying to fit in with the locals.

4 The Maid of Buttermere, Melvyn Bragg
Based on the true story of an innkeeper's beautiful daughter who is seduced by a bigamist.

5 The Grasmere Journals, Dorothy Wordsworth
A record of life at Dove Cottage, with lyrical observations of the Lakes.

6 Rogue Herries, Hugh Walpole
A passionate romance set in 18th-century Cumberland.

7 Unruly Times, A S Byatt
Byatt explores the relationship between the two great poets, Wordsworth and Coleridge.

8 Swallows and Amazons, Arthur Ransome
A rip-roaring children's classic set in the Lake District.

9 Recollections of the Lake Poets, Thomas de Quincey
Candid biographical essays on the Lakes' literary titans.

10 Postman Pat, John Cunliffe
The enchanting tales of a Lakes' postman and his cat.

Left **Crab apples, Egremont Crab Fair** Centre **Rushbearing** Right **Keswick's lakeside theatre**

Festivals and Events

1 Words by the Water

A 10-day literature festival is held in Keswick's lakeside theatre in March. Fay Weldon, Brian Keenan and local author Melvyn Bragg were in previous line-ups. The programme is packed with readings and lectures on a wide range of topics. ◎ *Theatre by the Lake, Keswick • Map S6 • www.wayswithwords.co.uk*

2 Cockermouth Georgian Fair

Held every even-numbered year in May, this fair celebrates Cockermouth's Georgian heyday, with a costume parade, Red Coat display, hurdy-gurdy music, morris dancing, sedan-chair racing and juggling in the streets. ◎ *Map C2 • www.cockermouth.org.uk/georgianfair*

3 Appleby Horse Fair

The little town of Appleby hosts this ancient fair for a week in early June. Begun in 1685, it is still a meeting point for the gypsy community; horses are washed in the River Eden, and then traded. Visitors can see beautiful painted wooden caravans during this fair. ◎ *Appleby • Map G2*

4 Rushbearing

Held in Ambleside in early July and in Grasmere on the closest Saturday to St Oswald's Day (Aug 5), this fascinating archaic ceremony dates back to a time when the earth floor of St Mary's was renewed with rushes. Children carry rush crosses round the village before laying them in the church.

5 Rydal Sheepdog Trials

For over a century, the Rydal Sheepdog Trials, held in August, have provided a test of skill for dogs and their handlers. Fell foxhounds are seen here along with working terriers and beagles. There is also a "crooks and sticks" competition for shepherds. ◎ *Map F5*

6 Lakeland Country Fair

Held in mid-August in Torver, near Coniston, this traditional fair has something for everyone, especially children. The events include a dog show, fell races, shows featuring lurchers, sheepdogs and terriers, and Cumberland Wrestling. There are also demonstrations on topics as varied as taxidermy and bee keeping. ◎ *Map L2 • www.lakelandcountryfair.co.uk*

Brightly painted caravans at Appleby Horse Fair

Cartmel Races

Enjoy a day out at the Cartmel Racecourse in May and during the August bank holiday weekend. Cartmel also provides a huge fairground with food and drink stands as well as entertainment for all ages. ✆ Map N4
• www.cartmel-racecourse.co.uk

Lake District Summer Music

Every August, this 3-week festival of classical music is held in a range of venues throughout the Lake District. It attracts renowned as well as emerging international musicians. ✆ www.ldsm.org.uk

Cumberland wrestling

Egremont Crab Fair

This fair has been held at harvest time (around mid-September) almost continuously since 1267. The name refers to the tradition of handing out crab apples to fair goers. It also features Cumberland wrestling, gurning (pulling funny faces through a horse's collar), and horn-blowing. ✆ Map B5
• www.egremontcrabfair.com

World's Biggest Liar

Locals and a few visitors compete each November to tell the most entertaining tall tale to an exacting pub audience. There are few rules, but politicians and lawyers are not permitted to join. ✆ Bridge Inn, Santon Bridge • Map C6

Top 10 Arts Venues

Brewery Arts Centre
A hot spot for creativity, with cinemas, a theatre and exhibition space (see p12).

Theatre by the Lake
This modern glass theatre in Keswick has a strong repertory programme (see p28).

Rosehill Theatre
A venue featuring music, theatre, film, comedy and dance. ✆ Whitehaven • Map A4
• 01946 692422

The Coro
The grand Coronation Hall in Ulverston hosts all kinds of art events, ✆ Coronation Hall, County Square, Ulverston
• Map M4 • 01229 587140

The Old Laundry Theatre
Hosts theatre, music and film from Aug to Dec. ✆ Crag Brow, Bowness-on-Windermere
• Map N2 • 015394 88444
• Box Office 10am–5pm Mon–Sat

Zeffirelli's
Eclectic Zeff's is a cinema and restaurant, but also has weekend jazz nights (see p16).

The Kirkgate Centre
An impressive venue in Cockermouth, showcasing art house films and theatre.
✆ Map C2 • 01900 826448
• Open 10am–1pm Mon–Fri

Upfront Puppet Theatre
A fantastic puppet theatre located in a 17th-century farm. ✆ Near Hutton in the Forest, Penrith • Map G2 • 017684 84538
• Open 10:30am–4:30pm daily

Alhambra Cinema
This little Keswick cinema is a historic gem (see p29).

Fellini's
Ambleside's second art house cinema. ✆ Church Street
• Map F5 • 015394 33845

Left **Stained glass, Cartmel Priory** Centre **St Michael's** Right **St Olaf's**

Churches and Abbeys

1 Shap Abbey
Sitting on the banks of the Lowther, the ruins of Shap Abbey create a harmonious if slightly melancholy picture. A 16th-century tower still stands, but little remains of the 13th-century buildings – church, cloister and dormitories. The abbey was begun in the late-12th-century by the Premonstratensians (a Catholic religious order), also known as the White Canons for the colour of their robes.
⬡ 2 miles (3 km) W of Shap • Map H4

2 St Michael's
Perched above Hawkshead, St Michael's was built in 1500 and boasts a 21-m (70-ft) high nave with impressive pillars and painted arches. As a schoolboy, Wordsworth liked to while away time here, enjoying the sweeping views of Esthwaite Water and the Langdale pikes.
⬡ Hawkshead • Map M2

3 St Kentigern
The origins of this church on the fringes of Keswick are of great antiquity, with the present

building dating back to the 16th century. It incorporates a mosaic floor, 12th-century glass, an ancient sundial and 21 Tudor "consecration crosses" that mark the places where the bishop sprinkled holy water. The church was restored in the mid-19th century by architect George Gilbert Scott.
⬡ Crosthwaite • Map D3

4 Cartmel Priory
This Augustine Priory has been a place of worship for 800 years. Many features remain from the 1400s, including the square belfry tower, the rose window and the choir stalls. There is also a 20th-century sculpture, *They Fled by Night*, by Josefina de Vasconcellos.
⬡ Priest Lane, Cartmel • Map N4
• www.cartmelpriory.org.uk

5 St Olaf's
This is England's smallest – as well as one of its most atmospheric – churches. The little interior of St Olaf's is white-washed with heavy beams overhead, said to have come from Viking longships. Look out for the representation of the craggy Napes Needle (a pinnacle on Great Gable) etched into one of the windows. You can also visit the graves of climbers who died in early ascents of the surrounding peaks *(see p27)*.

Interior, St Kentigern

6 St James's

This pretty country church sits above the picturesque village of Buttermere. The southern window of St James's is dedicated to writer and walker Alfred Wainwright. From here, you can look out at Haystacks, Wainwright's favourite Lakeland hike. There has been a chapel here since the early 16th century, but the present building was constructed in 1840. ◈ Buttermere • Map C4

St James's Church

7 St Catherine's

Sitting within walking distance of Dalegarth, at the end of the Ravenglass & Eskdale line (see p53), St Catherine's dates back to the 12th-century. Look out for the octagonal font, decorated with stylized marigolds, inside this plain but handsome country church. ◈ Near Boot, Eskdale • Map K1

Gravestone, St Catherine's

8 Furness Abbey

The extensive and lovely red sandstone ruins of Furness Abbey are spread over a verdant site in what Wordsworth described in his epic poem, The Prelude as the "vale of nightshade". The abbey, located on the outskirts of Barrow-in-Furness, was founded by the Savigniac monks, came to the Cistercians in the mid-12th century, and was destroyed during the Reformation, although some fine stonework is still intact. ◈ 3 km (2 miles) N of Barrow-in-Furness • Map L5 • 01229 823420 • Apr–Sep: 10am–5pm Thu–Mon, Oct–Mar: 10am–4pm Sat & Sun; call before visiting to check if open • Adm • www.english-heritage.org.uk

9 St Martin's Church

This lovely and plain little 16th-century church sits on a quiet lane above the east shore of Ullswater: it is backed by a yew tree that may be 1,300 years old. The best approach to St Martin's is from Howtown, a stop-off point on the steamer route. ◈ Ullswater • Map F4

10 St Andrew's

This ancient church has plenty of treasures, including a Viking monument and the four bear statues that guard each corner of the churchyard. Dating from the 12th century, the church was restored in the 15th century, and again more recently by the Victorians. ◈ Dacre • Map G3

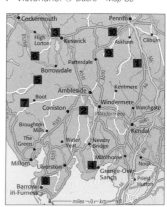

Left **Children's Garden, Dalemain** Centre **Fell Foot Park and Lake Windermere** Right **Mirehouse**

🔟 Gardens

1 Graythwaite Hall Garden

This late-Victorian garden in a wooded valley was designed by Thomas Mawson. It is at its best in spring, when you can wander the woodland paths and see the azaleas and rhododendrons in bloom. ◈ *Graythwaite, Ulverston • Map N3 • 015395 31248 • Open Apr–Oct: 10am–6pm daily • Adm • www.graythwaitehall.co.uk*

Roses, Brockhole Gardens

2 Sizergh Castle

The spacious and romantic gardens at Sizergh include ancient woodland, abundant orchards and a limestone rock garden, as well as stretches carpeted with wildflowers, a water garden and an impressive collection of ferns *(see p12)*.

3 Brockhole Gardens

This lovely Arts & Crafts garden is structured with terraces that look towards

Muncaster Castle Gardens

Windermere and the Langdale Pikes. It features old-fashioned roses, a wildflower meadow, a kitchen garden and herbaceous borders. A mild microclimate means that unusual plants such as the Handkerchief Tree, Chilean Lantern Tree and Kashmir Cyprus can flourish. ◈ *Brockhole, Windermere • Map N1 • 015394 46601 • Open 9am–dusk daily • www.lakedistrict.gov.uk*

4 Fell Foot Park

A beautiful Victorian park land sloping down to Lake Windermere, Fell Foot Park is awash with daffodils in spring. The crenellated boathouse here adds architectural interest. Get a different perspective on the park by hiring a rowing boat and exploring the lake *(see p11)*.

5 Mirehouse

This garden dates back to the late-18th century, as the mighty Scottish pines along the driveway testify. Beneath the trees, clusters of hydrangeas and rhododendrons add colour. At the front of the house is an ancient wildflower garden. There is also a bee garden complete with hives, and an orchard full of Cumbrian fruit trees *(see p91)*.

6 Muncaster Castle

A walk down the driveway at Muncaster has an Alice in Wonderland feel: visitors are

Lush gardens, Holker Hall

dwarfed by the enormous hardwood trees, planted in the late-18th century. Visit in April and May to see the similarly monumental rhododendrons and azaleas of the Sino-Himalayan gardens in flower; there is also a collection of magnolias, camellias and maples *(see p68)*.

Holker Hall
The gardens at Holker Hall beautifully combine structured and formal elements, such as the long, stepped water cascades with patches of ancient wood-land. One of the great treasures of the grounds is the 16th-century Great Holker Lime which, with an 8-m (26-ft) girth, is one of the oldest and biggest lime trees in the country *(see p68)*.

Children's Garden, Dalemain
The symmetrical pink ashlar façade of Dalemain is softened by tall clusters of herbaceous plants. Explore a little further and find hidden treasures for children that include a bed planted with animal-and bird-related plants such as squirrel-grass and cranesbill, and a large mound of earth shaped to resemble a sleeping giant. ◈ *Dalemain • Map G3 • 017684 86450 • Gardens open end Mar– end Oct: 10:30am–5pm Sun–Thu • Adm • www.dalemain.com*

Brantwood
Many elements of the wonderfully imaginative gardens at Brantwood were the creation of Ruskin himself *(see p23)*. The Zig-Zaggy, for example, was structured to depict Dante's journey to paradise, while Ruskin's favourite, the Professor's Garden, has plants that benefit both body and soul *(see p24)*.

Levens Hall
This unusual garden in the grounds of Elizabethan Levens Hall is a remarkable relic from the past: it is a flamboyant topiary garden, created in 1694. Other historic elements in the garden include the nuttery, a herb garden and dense herbaceous borders *(see p68)*.

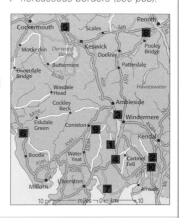

Left **Interior, Dalemain** Centre **Blackwell** Right **Collection of books, Mirehouse**

Top 10 Castles and Houses

1 Kendal Castle
There is no mistaking the strategic significance Kendal Castle had when it was built at the end of the 12th century – it commands an epic view over Kendal and the surrounding hills. The castle has been ruined since Tudor times, but the steep walls still give a vivid feeling of scale and power *(see p12)*.

2 Mirehouse
Secluded and grand, Mirehouse features a wonderful collection of furniture, portraits and letters written by past owners to Carlyle, Tennyson and Wordsworth. Built in 1666 and sold in 1688, Mirehouse has stayed in the same family ever since *(see p91)*.

3 Muncaster Castle
This eccentric and splendid home has been occupied by the Pennington family since 1208. It is said to be one of Britain's most haunted castles, with much of the trouble being caused by 15th-century court jester Tom Skelton – you can check out his malevolent features in a large-scale portrait *(see p68)*.

4 Dalemain
Dalemain has a magnificent symmetrical Georgian façade, behind which lie more irregular and intriguing Tudor and medieval buildings – in fact, the origins of this family home go back to the Saxon period. The interiors are decked out with portraits and hand-painted Oriental wallpaper, and there is also an interesting collection of antique toys and doll houses *(see p47)*.

5 Levens Hall
The weathered but lovely Elizabethan exterior of Levens Hall conceals a much older medieval tower. The interiors are wonderfully preserved, with

Muncaster Castle

their fine Italian plasterwork, leather panelling and stained glass. There is a also collection of clocks and delicate miniatures, and the topiary gardens are world famous *(see p68)*.

Holker Hall
Holker Hall is still home to the Cavendish family, and the west wing, constructed in the Victorian period in lavish Elizabethan-Gothic style, is the one part of the house that is open to the public. Visitors can explore the sumptuous library and bedrooms and climb the very grand cantilevered wooden staircase *(see p68)*.

Brantwood
John Ruskin's lakeside villa is a symphony of light and colour and a showcase of his art collection; start your visit by watching the video about the critic and painter's life and work. The stunning views of Coniston are at their best in the Turret Room, where the aged Ruskin sat in his bath chair *(see p24)*.

Blackwell
This Arts & Crafts creation, built by M H Baillie-Scott in 1900, is wonderfully preserved, with its panelling, wall-hangings, bold stained glass and elongated furnishings intact. Blackwell also serves as a showcase for contemporary crafts and sculpture *(see p10)*.

Sizergh Castle
Constructed around a blunt medieval tower, the rambling Tudor

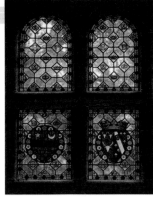

Stained glass, Holker Hall

buildings of Sizergh have been the home of the Strickland family for a remarkable 750 years. Inside you will find ancient family portraits, Elizabethan paneling and fine French and English furniture. The castle's gardens are outstanding *(see p13)*.

Egremont Castle
This Norman castle at Egremont sits on a mound above the little medieval market town. Although the structure has been in ruins since the 16th century, remnants of the castle's imposing walls and gatehouse give some sense of its more illustrious past.
⊗ *Egremont • Map B5*

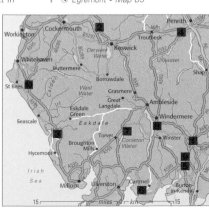

Left **Peel Island** Centre **Great North Swim** Right **Rydal Water**

🔟 Best Swims

1 Silecroft Beach
Tucked away in the south of the Lake District, this is a lovely sand and shingle beach backed by Black Combe Fell. Silecroft beach is great for a paddle and a swim, as well as for windsurfing, water-skiing, canoeing and a spot of sea-fishing. ❧ *Map K4*

2 High Dam
This deep tarn, which once powered the Stott Bobbin Mill *(see pp10–11)* is a peaceful place for a dip. Surrounded by larches and Scots pine, High Dam is located near the village of Finsthwaite, and reached on a footpath from the National Trust car park. ❧ *Finsthwaite • Map M3*

3 Wast Water
Brace yourself for some deep waters and for truly impressive views of the surrounding scree-covered slopes. Wast Water is 5-km (3-miles) long, so it provides a really stretching swim for strong swimmers. Warm up with pub grub at the Wasdale Head Inn *(see p117)*. ❧ *Map C5*

4 Peel Island, Coniston
Follow in the adventurous footsteps of the *Swallows and Amazons* brigade and paddle your canoe out to Peel Island – known as Wildcat Island in the books – for a swim in the cove in the chilly Coniston Water. ❧ *Map M3*

5 Rydal Water
Take a dip among the reed beds of Rydal Water, beloved of Wordsworth. The mountain views in this part of the Central Fells are unbeatable and make the swim truly memorable. ❧ *Map F5*

An idyllic view of Wast Water

River Esk, Eskdale

the southern end of Coniston Water. You can park in the Brown Howe car park for the relatively short walk to get here. ◎ Map L3

Blackmoss Pot
This deep natural pool is edged by high rocks, which brave swimmers can jump from. Blackmoss Pot also has a waterfall at each end. It is perfect for a summer wallow after a long hike in Borrowdale. All in all, a wonderfully secluded spot for a summer dip. ◎ Stonethwaite • Map D4

River Esk, Eskdale
The course of River Esk, framed by stone bridges, is punctuated by natural pools that are perfect for a dip on the rare but magical hot days in the Lakes. You can also fish here, and it is possible to canoe the course of the river. ◎ Map C6

St Bees Head
South of Whitehaven, St Bees features a wonderful long sandy beach, divided by wooden groynes. It is edged by St Bees Head, 6 km (4 miles) of red sandstone cliffs with colonies of puffins, razorbills and guillemots. The name derives from 7th-century St Bega, who founded a priory here. ◎ Map A4

Great North Swim
This is a terrific communal event – a 1.6-km (1-mile) open-water swim in Windermere. You are likely to be splashing alongside 6,000 others – there is an elite course for the pros, but swimmers of all abilities can join in. It takes place in September, so balmy temperatures are not guaranteed. ◎ Windermere • Map N1 • www. greatswim.org

Beacon Tarn
The hidden Beacon Tarn provides an outdoor swim for romantics and sweeping views of Coniston Water. Reachable only on foot, the tarn, reckoned to be the warmest swim in the Lakes, is located at

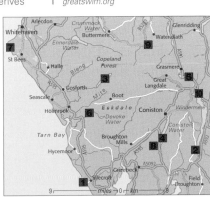

Left **Ullswater Steamer** Centre **Pier, Coniston Water** Right **Lakeside & Haverthwaite Railway**

🔟 Great Journeys

1 Steam Yacht Gondola

Take a trip on this elegant little pleasure steamer up Coniston Water. The 90-minute Explorer Cruise includes informed commentary on writer Arthur Ransome and art critic and social thinker John Ruskin. The Sunday morning Wild Cat Island Cruise makes a stop at Ruskin's home at Brantwood *(see p24)* and the Gothic country house Monk Coniston with its lovely walled garden *(see p25)*.

2 Windermere Cruise

All kinds of ferries ply the largest lake in the country, with stops at Waterhead, Bowness and Lakeside. This is a useful way of getting around, especially if you want to avoid the crowded roads. Take the Jazz Buffet Cruise with live performances by the New Hall Jazz Band for a laidback Lakes experience. Additionally, a small car ferry takes visitors straight across the lake from Bowness to Far Sawrey *(see p11)*.

Hardknott Roman Fort

3 Hardknott Pass

The name conveys something of the gritty adventure that driving on this steep road entails. The route links the two valleys of Eskdale and Langdale, but is more of a gear-grinding challenge rather than a short cut. Stop to see the impressive remains of the Hardknott Roman Fort *(see p32)*. 🕲 *Map D6*

4 Blea Tarn Road

This road enables you to do an 13-km (8-mile) circuit of Great and Little Langdale, one of the most scenic areas in the Lake District, with plenty of beautiful ghylls and tarns. Break your journey at Old Dungeon Ghyll where you can enjoy a walk as well as relax over a pint of beer and lunch at the Old Dungeon Ghyll Hotel *(see p18)*.

A ferry docked at the pier, Lake Windemere

Coniston Cruise

Take a trip in *Swallows and Amazons* country with the Coniston Launch service. It runs leisurely cruises as well as scheduled services for a quick but enjoyable journey across the lake. ✆ Coniston • Map M2 • 01768 77575 • Open daily mid-Mar–Oct, Sat–Sun Nov–mid-Mar • Adm • www.conistonlaunch.co.uk

Kirkstone Pass

This spectacular white-knuckle drive in the Lakes, between Ambleside and Patterdale, offers superb views in either direction. However, the steep gradients of this high pass make it tough going in bad weather. Take a break at the rambling, whitewashed Kirkstone Pass Inn. ✆ Map F5

Winding road through Kirkstone Pass

Ullswater Steamer

These red-funnelled steamers are an essential part of the Ullswater landscape. The fleet includes *Lady of the Lake*, believed to be the oldest working passenger vessel in the world – it has been operating since 1877 – and the *Raven*, which took to the water in 1889. These historic steamers connect Glenridding in the south with Howtown, the half-way point, and the village of Pooley Bridge in the north *(see p83)*.

Ravenglass & Eskdale Railway

Ravenglass & Eskdale Railway

Built to carry iron ore, this heritage steam-railway line follows a very scenic route, from the coast to the heart of the National Park. Starting from Ravenglass in the west, it trundles via Barrow Marsh, Rock Fell, Eskdale and Dalegarth. ✆ Ravenglass • Map J2/K2 • 01229 717171 • www.ravenglass-railway.co.uk

Lakeside & Haverthwaite Railway

A picturesque little branch line which makes a 6-km (4-mile) journey to connect the tiny village of Haverthwaite with the southern end of Lake Windermere. Here you can leave the train and continue your journey by steamer on the water *(see p10)*.

Cumbrian Coast Line

A little off the tourist trail, the Cumbrian Coast railway line allows you to explore intriguing destinations such Barrow-in Furness, Millom, Ravenglass, St Bees and Whitehaven. The journey ends at Carlisle, where visitors can link up with mainline services to major UK stations. ✆ www.nationalrail.co.uk

Left **Exterior, Black Bull** Centre **Label for a Local Beer** Right **Interior, Watermill Inn**

🔟 Best Pubs and Inns

1 Hikers Bar, Old Dungeon Ghyll Hotel

A rugged bar where muddy boots will not keep you from crossing the threshold. There are open fires in winter and a stone terrace for the summers. Real ales, Scotch whiskies and large restorative portions of pub grub are served here and the fell-foot location is superb *(see p79)*.

2 Black Bull

A 400-year-old coaching inn located under the iconic Old Man of Coniston, the Black Bull has a rich history. De Quincey stopped here en route to meeting Wordsworth and it has also hosted Coleridge and Turner. It serves home-brewed ales, including Bluebird Bitter and Winter Warmer Blacksmiths Ale *(see p70)*.

3 The Hole in t'Wall

Pints have been served at this rambling and characterful old place a short walk from Lake Windermere since 1612. The

Beer tap at Ritson's Bar

very Cumbrian name derives from the fact that a past landlord used to hand beer through a hole in the wall to his neighbour, the blacksmith *(see p70)*.

4 Ritson's Bar, Wasdale Head Inn

A true Lakeland walkers' bar located in the lovely Wasdale Valley, Ritson's is traditional and cosy. The filling bar meals and real ales will revive you after a hike. There are cheerful log stoves in winter, and outdoor tables by a little stream in summer *(see p103)*.

5 Bar at The Kings Arms Hotel

Another venerable Lake District Inn, located in the wonderfully preserved village of Hawkshead, the Kings Arms is 500 years old, but has been sensitively modernized. There are nine cosy rooms if you fancy staying over. Real ales, malt whiskies and a beer garden complete the picture *(see p70)*.

Visitors enjoying afternoon pints, Hole in t'Wall

6 The Masons Arms, Cartmel Fell

The atmospheric Masons Arms offers glorious views over Winster valley. It also has five draught ales and a huge range of bottled beers. The imaginative food makes good use of seasonal and local produce *(see p70)*.

Sun Inn

Sun Inn, Crook

A fine old whitewashed pub, the Sun Inn is located in a row of 18th-century millworkers' cottages. It features the requisite open fires and stone floors, tasty traditional Lakeland food and local beers and ales *(see p70)*.

Eagle & Child Inn, Staveley

Located on the banks of the River Kent, this lovely village inn has a large garden and is a great stop for walkers along the Kent. The list of real ales is impressive, and candles in the evening add to the ambience *(see p70)*.

Cuckoo Brow Inn

A quiet Lake District inn located in an old stable block, nestled in the village of Far Sawrey. From here it is only a short walk to the famous home that once belonged to Beatrix Potter and that is now run by the National Trust. Hearty food is served in the cosy bar and ales are sourced from local breweries – Ulverston provides a new one to try each month. Guests can explore the historical features of the inn *(see p70)*.

Watermill Inn, Ings

An award-winning pub with a microbrewery that produces Collie Wobbles, amongst numerous other fine ales. The owners pride themselves on their dog-friendliness *(see p70)*.

Top 10 Breweries

Whitehaven Brewing Company
This brewery makes ales that are not treated with chemicals. ◈ *Croasdale Farm, Ennerdale* • Map B4 • 01946 861755

Jennings Castle Brewery
This 19th-century brewery uses water from its own well. ◈ *Brewery Lane, Cockermouth* • Map C2 • 0845 1297185

Hardknott Brewery
A great artisanal micro-brewery. ◈ *Near Hardknott Pass* • Map D6 • 01229 779309

Ulverston Brewing Company
A quality company that stocks the surrounding pubs. ◈ *59 Urswick Road, Ulverston* • Map M4 • 01229 584280

Keswick Brewing Company
Lovingly created ales, all with the prefix "Thirst": Thirst Run, Thirst Fall and others *(see p95)*.

Hawkshead Brewery
This brewery produces the Hawkshead Bitter and Lakeland Gold *(see p70)*.

Cumbrian Legendary Ales
Their ales include Loweswater Gold and Grasmoor Dark Ale. ◈ *Old Hall Brewery, Hawkshead* • Map M2 • 01539 436436

Coniston Brewery
Cask-conditioned, award-winning ales are created here. ◈ *Coppermines Road, Coniston* • Map M2 • 015394 41133

Barngates Brewery
Water from a nearby tarn is used in the production of the ales. ◈ *Barngates, Ambleside* • Map F5 • 015394 36575

Bitter End Brewery
A terrific little brewery with great seasonal ales *(see p96)*.

Left **Ravenglass & Eskdale Railway** Centre **Ullswater Steamer** Right **Honister Slate Mine**

TOP 10 **Children's Attractions**

1 Ravenglass & Eskdale Railway

Nothing thrills most small children more than a ride on a steam train. Adults are catered for on this journey too by the magnificent scenery, which the miniature locomotives trundle through, from Ravenglass on the coast to the bottom of the mighty Eskdale Valley *(see p53)*.

2 The Lakeland Climbing Centre

Before your offspring are tempted by real-life crags, get them in training at this well-run and enjoyable indoor centre with its 25-m (82-ft) high climbing wall, cave area, as well as bouldering rooms. The centre runs 90-minute taster sessions, more involved classes and outdoor trips, too *(see p12)*.
ⓢ www.kendalwall.co.uk

The Lakeland Climbing Centre

3 Honister Slate Mine

Located at the summit of the steep Honister Pass, the slate mine offers underground tours that are an eye-opener for kids – they can learn how young children laboured in the mine in times past. The drive to get here is an adventure in itself. ⓢ *Honister Pass, between Buttermere and Borrowdale* • *Map D4* • *017687 77230* • *Open daily; tours: 10:30am, 12:30pm, 2pm & 3:30pm* • *Adm* • *www.honister-slate-mine.co.uk*

4 Lake District Visitor Centre

The visitor centre in Windermere is all set up for children: with an adventure playground complete with tree top trek, indoor soft play area, mini-golf and boat hire. There are also exhibits on the flora and fauna and the geology of the region, with plenty of events geared towards children *(see p11)*.

5 Ullswater Steamer

There are plenty of options for lake-bound trips, but the Ullswater Steamers with their picture-book scarlet funnels are particularly appealing for children. Download activity sheets from the website to maximize the educational value of your outing *(see p53)*.

6 Milking at Low Sizergh Farm

The second-storey café at Sizergh looks down at the milking shed, where you can see the organic herd ambling in for milking each afternoon. This and the farmyard trail with its chicks, pigs, cows and ancient woodland make for an educational yet irresistible children's outing. ✆ Low Sizergh Barn, Sizergh • Map P3 • 015395 60426 • Open 9am–5pm daily • www.lowsizerghbarn.co.uk

The World Owl Centre
Children and adults alike will be mesmerized by the car-lamp orange eyes and vast scale of eagle owls when seen at close range, but there are more than

The World Owl Centre

40 different types of owl in this conservation centre. During afternoon talks you can find out about the birds and watch them in flight. ✆ Muncaster Castle, Muncaster, Ravenglass • Map J2 • 01229 717614 • Meet the Birds: Apr–Oct 2:30pm • www.muncaster.co.uk

Fell Foot Park
This park has expansive grounds in which to stroll, play games and have picnics as well as an adventure playground for children. At the castellated boathouse on the shores of Windermere you can hire rowing boats – it also serves as a café (see p10). ✆ www.nationaltrust.org.uk

Rufty Tuftys Indoor Activity Centre

Rufty Tuftys
This large indoor activity centre just outside Ambleside provides a safe, clean and stimulating environment for children aged up to 11 years. Parents can relax and enjoy coffee and cake in the café while their children play. ✆ Rothay Road, Ambleside • Map N1 • 015394 39906 • Open 10am–5:30pm daily • www.ruftytuftys.co.uk

Go Ape
A challenging, not to say slightly scary, system of zip wires, ladders, swings and platforms which takes you high above the ground and through the tree canopy. There is a minimum age of 10, and height restrictions also apply. Back on the ground, look out for the striking wooden sculptures dotting the forest. ✆ Grizedale Forest • Map M2 • 0845 6439215 • Open Apr–Oct: Wed–Mon, Nov & Feb: Sat & Sun • Adm • www.goape.co.uk

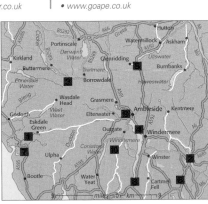

Left **Great Gable** Centre **Grizedale Forest** Right **The Coffin Trail**

🔟 Best Walks

1 Helvellyn

As England's third-highest peak, Helvellyn should not be approached lightly. The narrow Striding Edge route makes for a challenging though exhilarating scramble, and is only for experienced and well-equipped hikers. Wordsworth, who climbed this mountain regularly, wrote of the death of a walker on Striding Edge. ✪ Map E4

Signage, The Coffin Trail

2 Ambleside to Skelwith Bridge

This lovely route is a good starter before you attempt more demanding Lakeland hikes. Suitable for people of all ages, it winds its way from Ambleside via Loughrigg Tarn to Skelwith Bridge, which is a good place to stop for a pint of beer. All along the way, the Langdale Pikes provide a magnificent back-drop. ✪ Map N1–M1

3 The Coffin Trail

This rather grim sounding route was taken by coffin bearers shouldering their load across the hills to St Oswald's in Grasmere for burial. The woodland paths link Grasmere with Rydal and on to Ambleside, and make for a secluded and not too demanding hike (see p8).

4 Aira Force

A steep, lovely and fairly short walk from the shores of Ullswater leads up to the magnificent 20-m (65-ft) drop of Aira Force (waterfall). Visitors may spot red squirrels among the attractive woodland paths here. There is also a simple tearoom at hand. ✪ Map F4

5 Grizedale Forest

Located on the eastern shores of Coniston Water, Grizedale Forest comprises 6,000 acres (2,400 ha) of larch, oak, spruce and pine woodland. A haven for red deer and roe deer, this forest also features a terrific sculpture trail with works created by British

Cyclists on the Ambleside to Skelwith Bridge route

Path up the Old Man of Coniston

artists such as Andy Goldsworthy and David Nash. The walking routes are marked with specific colour codes. ◎ *Map M2*

Scafell Pike

The highest mountain in England, Scafell can be approached from various directions such as Wasdale, Seathwaite Farm in Borrowdale or the Old Dungeon Ghyll Hotel. Be sure you are equipped to tackle this mountain. ◎ *Map D5*

Great Gable

One of the Lake District's iconic climbs, Great Gable has a distinctive pyramidical peak. On a clear day, the summit offers stunning views of Wasdale, Scafell and Scafell Pike. A classic route up the mountain is via Seathwaite. ◎ *Map D5*

Easedale Tarn

Hike from Grasmere up the fellsides to Easedale Tarn, a lake that sits among some forbidding peaks. A round trip takes about 3 hours, and the ascent is pretty steep, but it is wonderfully peaceful. ◎ *Map E5*

The Old Man of Coniston

Walking guru Wainwright wrote about the slate mines scarring the Old Man of Coniston, and visitors can still see the remnants of mining works here. The mountain has epic views out over Coniston Water, and its well-worn trails make it a favourite with hikers (see p24).

Crinkle Crags

The profile of these peaks forms five distinct "crinkles", which make for a pretty strenuous hike. This trek is best attempted on a clear day, both for the views and for safety. Most walkers start their ascent from Old Dungeon Ghyll. ◎ *Map D5*

Low cloud over Easedale Tarn

Left **Sharrow Bay** Centre **Afternoon tea at Faeryland** Right **Sizergh Barn afternoon tea cakes**

Venues for Afternoon Tea

Lucy's on a Plate
This Ambleside café is not the place for a dainty afternoon tea: you can have a tiered plate of fruit cake and scones, a slab of sticky lemon cake, plus a pot of Lakeland tea. It is the perfect restorative boost after a long hike. *Church Street, Ambleside • Map F5 • 015394 31191*

Tiered plate of Cakes, Lucy's

Hat Trick Café, Low Newton
A unique place, the Hat Trick Café is located inside Yew Tree Barn. The cosy café, with its red chequered tablecloths, has a 1930s vibe, and every surface is hung with vintage hats. Proprietor Sam bakes treats such as scones and moist ginger cake *(see p69)*.

The Tea Garden, Keswick
A pretty landscaped spot for a cup of tea in the small cottage garden of a free-range farm, which is designed for people who are walking through the valley. The Tea Garden is very popular, offering home-made cakes dished up on locally made ceramics. *Low Bridge End Farm, St John's-in-the-Vale, Keswick • Map P3 • 017687 79242*

Gillam's Tearoom
At Gillam's in Ulverston they are tea purists, serving single-estate loose-leaf teas from all over the globe. It is a traditional tearoom that was founded way back in 1892. Gilliam's Tearoom has an ethical outlook and the baked goodies are all home-made and made from organic and Fairtrade products. *64 Market Street, Ulverston • Map M4 • 01229 587564*

Blackwell Tearoom
This light-filled modern tearoom at Blackwell is an elegant place for a quintes-sential English afternoon tea with a pot of tea with scones, fruit jam and freshly whipped cream. In summer, you can take your tea outside, and admire the white-washed gabled exterior of M H Baillie Scott's beautiful Arts & Crafts house *(see p10)*. *Bowness-on-Windermere • Map N2 • 015394 46139*

Interior, Blackwell Tearoom

Faeryland, Grasmere

An enchanting summertime option, Faeryland is an outdoor tearoom where you can combine a cup of loose-leaf tea with rowing a boat on Grasmere. A brightly painted Romany caravan completes the picture. They have a choice of 48 teas including their own blends and you can buy a tin of Faeryland tea to take away. ◐ *The lakeshore, Grasmere • Map E5 • 015394 35060*

Afternoon tea, Broadoaks Country House Hotel

Linthwaite House Hotel

A fine country-house hotel with an attractive hilltop setting overlooking Windermere, the Linthwaite has a serious approach to afternoon tea. There are more modest options, but the blow-out "Grand" afternoon tea includes a glass of champagne, Cartmel valley smoked salmon sandwiches, lemon drizzle cake and ginger cake *(see p114)*.

Sharrow Bay

Another upmarket and traditional Lakes hotel, sitting right on the shores of Ullswater, Sharrow Bay also dishes up an opulent afternoon tea. Toasted teacakes, dainty sandwiches and cream cakes are among the delicacies on offer. Later, take a stroll in their woodland garden and admire the lake views *(see p114)*.

Broadoaks Country House Hotel, Troutbeck

Once a hunting lodge, today Broadoaks is a luxurious property that serves tea either by the fire in the Music Room dating back to 1904, or on the terrace where Mick Jagger and various members of The Beatles once had a two-week jamming session. The tiered treats include Victoria sponge, tea loaf and scones with whipped cream and organic jam, all served on pretty, traditional china. ◐ *Bridge Lane, Troutbeck • Map N1 • 015394 45566*

Low Sizergh Barn

Enjoy your tea with a different kind of view; the café looks out onto the farm's milking shed so you can see exactly where the organic cream on your scones comes from. Children adore it, the home-made food hits the spot and you can end your visit by taking the farm trail to see the animals and the vegetable garden *(see p13)*.

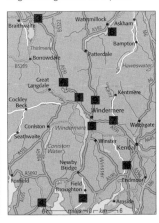

AROUND THE LAKE DISTRICT

THE LAKE DISTRICT'S TOP 10

Left **Gift shop, Blackwell** Centre **Pier, Bowness-on-Windermere** Right **Troutbeck**

Windermere and the South

The southern Lakes are very diverse, with the handsome town of Kendal forming the gateway to the area. Beyond Kendal lies Windermere – the name of both the bustling town and the huge lake, dotted with islands and ringed by historic houses such as Arts and Crafts Blackwell. A little car ferry takes you across the lake to Beatrix Potter's home at Near Sawrey, from where you can access picturesque Hawkshead. It is a region of impressive mountains but one of its lesser-known delights is a series of interesting coastal settlements.

St Michael's Church, Hawkshead

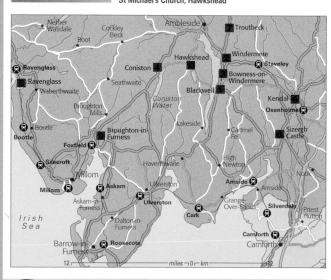

Preceding pages **Hill Top, Beatrix Potter's house, Near Sawrey**

Blackwell

A candidate for the most beautiful and best preserved Arts and Crafts house anywhere in the country, Blackwell was completed in 1900. The vast wood-panelled great hall has a minstrels' gallery, but it is free of twee medievalism. The lines are simple and elegant and there is wonderful furniture

Carved fireplace at Blackwell

throughout the house, plus well-chosen temporary exhibitions of historical and modern arts and crafts. Blackwell has all this plus an excellent shop selling pottery, art books, silver, glass, wood and metalwork as well as a fine café *(see p10)*.

Windermere

Windermere was a Victorian boom town, with rich industrialists coming in by train loads to build grand villas and stone mansions, many of which have now been converted into B&Bs. Although there are no unmissable sights here, it is a good place to stock up for a self-catering trip, and you could also

Coniston Water

stretch your legs in preparation for tougher fell climbs by walking up to Orrest Head, where you will be rewarded with panoramic views of the lake. ✎ *Map N2*

Bowness-on-Windermere

Cheery Bowness sits south of Windermere on the lake shore, and is the jumping off point for boat trips, whether you want a jazz cruise or a jaunt in a canoe. With more of an inviting feel to it than Windermere town, Bowness-on-Windermere is a good place for a walk along the shore or to visit the gift shops. The Windermere Steamboat Museum *(see pp10–11)* is a big draw for boat enthusiasts as well as kids – it has long been in redevelopment, but they run limited tours for interested visitors: just contact them in advance. ✎ *Map N2*

Coniston

An ancient copper-mining village, Coniston has more of a rugged feel to it than the eastern settlements. It sits at the head of the lake, from where you can make a boat trip to Brantwood *(see p24)*. This is also the starting point for walks up the craggy Old Man of Coniston, and offers good accommodation in old stone cottages. ✎ *Map M2*

Ravenglass & Eskdale Railway

Beatrix Potter

Potter (1866–1943) came from a wealthy but repressive family. In her thirties she wrote the *Tale of Peter Rabbit*, followed by more than twenty books, bringing her wide fame and independence. The key to the books' success are their delicate illustrations, and the fact that they are far from saccharine – Mr McGregor did put Peter's dad in a pie and eat him.

5 Ravenglass

Coastal Ravenglass is located at the estuary of the Esk, Mite and Irt rivers. It presents steep façades and high stone walls to the sea, which withdraw to reveal mud flats, tangled ropes and rusting anchors. The village with its terraced 19th-century cottages is well worth a look, as are the remains of a Roman bathhouse. It is also the starting point for one of the Lakes' most delightful attractions: the little steam trains of the Ravenglass & Eskdale Railway *(see p53)*. Map J2

6 Kendal

For a small town, Kendal has some pretty big attractions. There is the first-rate Abbot Hall Art Gallery with its collection of Romney portraits and contemporary art shows, the excellent and evocative Museum of Lakeland Life, the imposing ruins of a 12th-century hilltop castle and the buzzing Brewery Arts Centre. The town's warren of back streets conceals some great eating places, such as the Waterside Wholefood café by the river *(see p71)*.

Sculpture, Abbot Hall Art Gallery

7 Troutbeck

Just east of Windermere, the village of Troutbeck is the best place to see vernacular Lakes architecture: bulky stone bank barns, porches made of slabs of thin slate and impressive farmhouses with distinctive round chimneys. You can study this style up close at Townend *(see p10)*, a remarkably well-preserved farmhouse with its original furniture still intact. Built in 1626, the house was in the same family for more than 300 years until it was acquired by the National Trust in the 1940s. Map N1

8 Sizergh Castle

This fabulous castle was constructed around a medieval pele (solar tower), the solid core of which is now a rambling and absorbing building. The home of the Strickland family (they currently go by the name of Hornyhold-Strickland) for 800 years, it has an ancestral portrait from 1600, plus a few Romneys as well as glamorous Victorian and Edwardian paintings of the family. Guides offer architectural information and interesting

Main square, Broughton-in-Furness

anecdotes about the castle and its inhabitants, and the beautiful grounds include a limestone rock garden *(see p13)*.

Broughton-in-Furness
It is worth a detour from the usual tourist route to see Broughton-in-Furness, whose huge square of Georgian buildings feels disproportionate for a small country town. The town's wealth derived from its status as a cattle and wool market. Broughton is a good alternative base to the more crowded settlements, as it provides good access for Coniston and Hawkshead to the northeast and the coast and Furness Abbey to the south. ❧ *Map L3*

Hawkshead
This gem of a village is protected from cars (the centre is pedestrianized) and comprised of cobbled lanes of low white-washed cottages, decked out with flowers in summer. Hawkshead's most famous attractions are Wordsworth's school *(see p20)* and the grand 15th-century St Michael's Church. Beatrix Potter fans should visit the gallery of her work on the main street. There is also an excellent pub here – the King's Arms *(see p70)*. ❧ *Map M2*

A Drive Around the Southern Lakes

Morning

🕐 From Bowness, take the short drive south to Arts and Crafts **Blackwell** *(see p10)*, an architectural marvel that you cannot miss. This is a good stop for a morning coffee at the **Tearoom** *(see p60)*. After this, continue south along the lake on the A592, then head west on the A590. Take a detour to the south (B5278) to see the grandiose gardens of **Holker Hall** *(see p68)*. This is also a good option for lunch, as there is a lovely café here and an excellent food hall, where you can buy all the picnic supplies you'll need. Take your lunch to the promenade at **Grange-over-Sands** just to the east of Holker Hall.

Afternoon

Make your way back on the A590, then take the A5092 and the A595 west to the handsome Georgian market town of **Broughton-in-Furness**. This is well worth a wander. Then travel north on the A593 to Coniston where you can either visit the **Ruskin Museum** *(see p24)*, or drive round the lake to visit Ruskin's home, **Brantwood** *(see p24)*, though be aware that the house and gardens merit at least an hour. **Jumping Jenny** *(see p71)* located in the former stables of Brantwood is great for tea. Back in the car, go east through Hawkshead and Sawrey, with a possible stop at Beatrix Potter's home at **Hill Top** *(see p10)*. From here, hop on to a ferry which will take you across the lake and back to Bowness-on-Windermere.

Left **Laurel and Hardy Museum, Ulverston** Centre **Interior, Muncaster Castle** Right **Holker Hall**

TOP 10 Best of the Rest

1 Cartmel
Tiny Cartmel boasts a huge 12th-century priory *(see p44)*, a Michelin-starred restaurant *(see p71)* and fine pubs. ◈ *Map N4*

2 Near Sawrey
This little hamlet's main attraction is Beatrix Potter's farm, Hill Top *(see p10)*, which she bought with proceeds from her stories. ◈ *Map M2*

3 Levens Hall
This ancient tower is surrounded by Elizabethan additions. It also has the oldest topiary gardens in the world and a lush bowling green *(see p12)*.

4 Lakeside & Haverthwaite Railway
A great outing for kids, who will love the short ride on these miniature steam trains *(see p10)*.

5 Ulverston
Little-visited Ulverston has some great restaurants and boutiques. The birthplace of Stan Laurel, it is home to the quirky Laurel and Hardy Museum *(see p34)*. ◈ *Map M4*

6 Muncaster Castle
This massive, brooding structure is said to be Britain's most haunted castle. The collection of family portraits is outstanding. ◈ *Ravenglass • Map J2 • 01229 717614 • Castle open: 12 noon–4:30pm, Sun–Fri; Gardens: 10:30am–6pm daily • Adm • www.muncaster.co.uk*

7 Lake District Visitor Centre
A visitor centre with displays and information on the flora and fauna of the Lakes, plus an Arts and Crafts garden. The adventure playground and soft play area make it great for kids *(see p11)*.

8 Holker Hall
High Victorian architecture and gardens, complete with a long cascade and statuary. ◈ *Cark-in-Cartmel, Near Grange-over-Sands • Map M4 • 01539 558328 • Open mid-Mar–Oct: 10:30am–5:30pm Sun–Fri • Adm • www.holker.co.uk*

9 Furness Abbey
The romantic red sandstone ruins, which were destroyed during the Reformation, provided inspiration to Wordsworth. It was once one of the grandest Cistercian abbeys in the country *(see p45)*.

10 Grange-over-Sands
This Edwardian resort features a long promenade with palm trees and abundant flowers. ◈ *Map N4*

Left **Steve Hicks Blacksmiths** Centre **Yew Tree Barn** Right **Kentmere Pottery**

🔟 Shops and Galleries

1 Museum of Lakeland Life and Industry Gift Shop

This shop offers pottery, local crafts, books on local design and history, traditional toys, cards and historic photographs of Cumbrian shepherds and local festivities *(see p13)*.

2 Booths, Windermere

Stock up with supplies for a camping or self-catering trip at this local northwest supermarket chain. ✆ *Victoria Street, Windermere • Map N2 • 015394 46114*

3 Steve Hicks Blacksmiths

This artisan blacksmith has an attractive workshop with products ranging from candle holders to swirly chairs and benches. ✆ *Near Orrest Head, Windermere • Map N2 • 015394 42619*

4 Kirkland Books

A long-established outlet specializing in first editions and old signed copies. Titles include works by Beatrix Potter and Wordsworth. ✆ *11 Collin Croft, Kendal • Map S2 • 0800 0112368*

5 Blackwell Shop

A great store for contemporary pottery, with vases, tiles, crockery and bowls. They also stock a good range of books on crafts and architecture *(see p10)*.

6 Low Sizergh Barn

This beautiful 18th-century barn sells local food – including their own organic produce – plus clothes, homeware, handmade paper, pottery, rugs and natural skincare products *(see p13)*.

7 Yew Tree Barn

Antiques, gifts and bric-a-brac cram this wooden barn. There is a section for reclaimed pieces including fireplaces, baths and artists' studios. Make time for a cuppa in its idiosyncratic café. ✆ *Low Newton • Map N4 • 015395 31498 • www.yewtreebarn.co.uk*

8 Kentmere Pottery

Gordon Fox sells his own pottery, decorated with seasonal flowers such as daffodils, from his studio by an ancient mill. Lamps, planters and chocolate dishes are available, as well as mugs and bowls. ✆ *Kentmere, near Kendal • Map P1 • 01539 821621 • Open 9am–5pm Mon–Fri*

9 Hawkshead Relish Company

A lip-smacking selection of relishes, chutneys and jams are sold here in a historic building in Hawkshead; they are also available throughout the Lakes. ✆ *The Square, Hawkshead • Map M2 • 015394 36614 • www.hawksheadrelish.com*

10 Two by Two

This boutique sells bright scarves and clothes made from natural fibres. There is also a great bookshop next door *(see p37)*. ✆ *52 Market Street, Ulverston • Map M4 • 01229 480 703 • www.twobytwoulverston.com*

Left **Beer taps at Watermill Inn** Centre **Hole in t'Wall sign** Right **Exterior of The Sun Inn**

🔟 Pubs and Inns

The Masons Arms
Stop off at the Masons Arms for fine ales, a friendly welcome, excellent food and views of the Winster Valley. The upstairs dining room is very elegant. ⬥ Strawbery Bank, Cartmel Fell • Map N4 • 01539 68486

Eagle & Child Inn
An archetypal village inn which sits on the River Kent in Staveley, the Eagle & Child's garden is lovely in the summer. Combine with a visit to the craft outlets at Mill Yard in the village. ⬥ Staveley • Map P2 • 01539 821320

The Hole in t'Wall
This atmospheric early 17th-century inn in Bowness is a short walk from Lake Windermere. Sit outside on the stone terrace or head for the beamed and panelled interior. ⬥ Lowside, Bowness • Map N2 • 015394 43488

Black Bull
The whitewashed Black Bull brews its own bitters and ales: it is the perfect refuge for a post-walk pint. ⬥ Yewdale Road, Coniston • Map M2 • 01539 441 335

The Sun
A Coniston classic, handily located at the base of the path to the Old Man of Coniston (see p24). The Sun has a spacious terrace and the bar serves eight ales on handpump. ⬥ Coniston • Map M2 • 015394 41248

Watermill Inn & Brewery
Watermill is an award-winning pub with its own microbrewery. Popular with beer aficionados and all those that enjoy a cosy, welcoming atmosphere. ⬥ Ings, near Windermere • Map N2 • 01539 821309

Sun Inn
Very much a traditional and largely unchanged village inn, the Sun Inn was converted from whitewashed mill workers' cottages. Although it is off the beaten track, it draws lots of visitors. ⬥ Crook • Map P2 • 01539 821351

The King's Arms Hotel
A 500-year old inn in the heart of Hawkshead, the King's Arms offers decent bar meals, real ales and a huge selection of malt whiskies. The beer garden is idyllic in summer. ⬥ Main Square, Hawkshead • Map M2 • 015394 36372

Hawkshead Brewery Beer Hall
Next door to legendary Wilf's Café, this stone-built beer hall is a great location to sample home-brewed ales. ⬥ Mill Yard, Staveley • Map P2 • 01539 822644

Cuckoo Brow Inn
A great place to stay or eat and a good base to visit key Lakeland tourist destinations such as Beatrix Potter's Hill Top Farm, which is within easy walking distance. ⬥ Far Sawrey • Map M2 • 015394 43425

Left **Main course, Miller Howe** Centre **Interior, Gilpin Lodge**

🔟 Places to Eat

Drunken Duck
The best of British food is
served in this country pub that
has had an upmarket makeover.
Mains include pan-fried duck
breast or loin of venison; there
are also vegetarian options.
◈ *Barngates, Ambleside • Map N1*
• 015394 36347 • ££££

Waterside Wholefood
This terrific vegetarian café
with a white-washed interior and
chunky wooden furniture sits on
a footpath by the river in heart of
Kendal and serves hearty food.
◈ *Kent View, Kendal • Map P2 • 01539
729743 • Closed Sun*

Jumping Jenny
Jenny's features a lovely old-
fashioned counter, succulent
cakes and a stone terrace – a wood-
burning stove is lit in winter. Sandwiches (nicknamed Brantwiches)
and filling pasta mains are served.
◈ *Brantwood • Map M2 • 015394 41715*

Wilf's Café
Set in a rambling former
wood mill on the Kent, Wilf's
serves up tasty and filling home-
made food, including big
breakfasts. ◈ *Mill Yard, Back Lane,
Staveley • Map P2 • 01539 822329*

Miller Howe
Superbly cooked and well
presented dishes that use local
meat are served here. Miller
Howe also offers exquisite
puddings. ◈ *Rayrigg Road, Windermere
• Map N2 • 01539 442536 • ££££*

Rustique
A smart deli and restaurant,
Rustique fuses modern British
cuisine with a more traditional
style. ◈ *1B Brogden St, Ulverston
• Map N4 • 01229 587373 • Closed
Sun–Mon • ££*

L'Enclume
Serving delicate, colourful
and delicious food, Michelin
starred L'Enclume has elegant
decor and attentive service.
◈ *Cavendish Street, Cartmel • Map M4
• 015395 36362 • Closed Mon–Tue • ££££*

The Brown Horse Inn
Terrific and tasty organic
pub food and beer from its own
micro-brewery. Book ahead for
dinner at weekends: this place is
very popular. ◈ *Sunny Bank Road,
Winster, Windermere • Map N2
• 015394 43443 • ££*

Gilpin Lodge
A sumptuous dining
experience in one of the most
elegant hotels in the Lakes.
Wonderful presentation and
service. ◈ *Crook Road, Windermere
• Map N2 • 015394 88818 • ££££*

Holbeck Ghyll Country House Hotel
This contender for the best
restaurant in the Lakes serves
delicious Michelin-starred food.
And all of this in a beautiful
setting with breathtaking views
of the Langdale Pikes. ◈ *Holbeck
Lane, Windermere • Map N2 • 015394
32375 • ££££*

Around the Lake District – Windermere and the South

Left **Daffodils** Centre **St Mary's Church, Ambleside** Right **Coffin Route, Rydal–Grasmere**

The Central Fells

THIS IS PERHAPS THE MOST ENCHANTING PART *of the Lake District, cut through by the magnificent Langdale Valley, where undulating stone walls climb the fells, giving way to steeper sterner mountains. At the valley bottom is the rushing River Brathay, edged with paths for walkers. The area is blessed with two lovely settlements: Ambleside, with its excellent restaurant scene and cinemas, and Grasmere, forever associated with Wordsworth. A classic time to visit the area is March, to see the daffodils as they come into full bloom – although be aware that snowstorms are still a distinct possibility at this time.*

Langdale Valley

Sights

1. Rydal Mount
2. Great Langdale
3. Elterwater
4. Chapel Stile
5. The Cumbria Way
6. Grasmere
7. Dove Cottage
8. Skelwith Bridge
9. Ambleside
10. Hardknott Pass

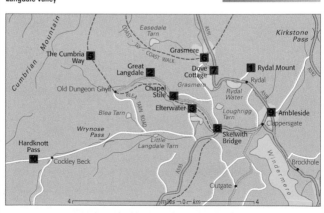

Preceding pages **Walkers near Haweswater**

Interior of Rydal Mount

Elterwater

This pretty little village sits on the river, and enjoys a wonderful aspect below the high fells. There's not much in the way of sights – just the village green and the convivial Britannia Inn – but it's an ideal tranquil base for walkers and cyclists. In summer you can take a seat outside the inn, and you'll be sure to fall into conversation with fellow walkers. Coniston and Grasmere are also good destinations for hikes from the village. ✎ Map E5

Rydal Mount

This was Wordsworth's home for the last 37 years of his life – the period when he was established and successful – and it is quite a contrast with the cramped conditions of Dove Cottage. In the library at Rydal Mount you can see the couch upon which the poet lay, and there is a good collection of paintings, letters and ephemera, including the poet's lunch box and his sister Dorothy's tiny shoes *(see pp20–21)*. ✎ www.rydalmount.co.uk

Great Langdale

Great Langdale offers the scenery of the Lake District on a grand scale: it is studded with stands of mature trees and the meadows are scattered with wild flowers during the summer. Around the valley rise iconic mountains such as Bowfell, Crinkle Crags and the Langdale pikes, landmarks in themselves, and in the history of climbing in this area. Their peaks are often shrouded by low clouds and these mountains have an imposing, sometimes formidable aspect. However, this is what makes them irresistible to the large numbers of walkers and climbers who come here. ✎ Map E5

Chapel Stile

This little quarry settlement is the next village up the valley from Elterwater, but it has more of a rugged feel, with its terraces of quarrymen's cottages and with the scars of the massive slate quarry visible above. The eponymous chapel is plain but attractive – have a look inside at the modern tapestry relating the history of the village. Brambles café *(see p81)* above the Co-op is a fine place for a coffee, while Wainwrights Inn *(see p79)* on the edge of Chapel Stile is an essential stop for walkers. ✎ Map E5

Chapel Stile

The Cumbria Way

The Cumbria Way

This long-distance path passes through stunning valleys in the Central Fells, on the 113-km (70-mile) route between Ulverston in the south and Carlisle in the north. It's a wonderful way to explore Coniston and the Langdale Valley – see the website for details on distances and accommodation. The flat stretch along the river between Elterwater and Chapel Stile is particularly attractive, and provides some gorgeous views.
⊗ Map E5 • www.thecumbriaway.info

Grasmere

There is a reason Grasmere gets overrun with visitors: it is probably the prettiest village in the Lakes, and is backed by some of the most magnificent fells. It is rich in Wordworthian associations: he is buried in the graveyard of St Oswald's – the interior of the church is worth a look too, for its impressive beamed roof. There are also plenty of cafés, a decent village pub, great accommodation and terrific walks *(see pp8–9)*.

Dove Cottage

Wordsworth's home from 1799 to 1808 is a richly evocative place, at once charming and plain. The family lived an austere life here – Walter Scott reported that they ate three meals a day, two of them porridge. Expert guides bring the place to life, while the adjoining museum has absorbing background on domestic life at Grasmere, and on the Romantic poets. There are wonderful portraits of the poet and of Byron, Coleridge and others, plus you can see William's court suit, panama hat, socks and toothscrapers *(see pp20–23)*.
⊗ www.wordsworth.org.uk

Skelwith Bridge

Skelwith Bridge, some 4.8 km (3 miles) west of Ambleside, sits at the end of the Langdale Valley and is the starting point for many walks in the area. It is a tiny, pretty place that clusters around the bridge over the Brathay – Chesters Café is a popular upmarket eating place, and you can buy items made from the distinctive local green slate at

Interior, Dove Cottage

Touchstone Interiors. A stroll up the river takes you to Skelwith Force (waterfall). ✣ *Map E6*

9 Ambleside

It is hard to resist the laidback charms of Ambleside, a little Lakes town with an enjoyably sophisticated atmosphere. There are lively cafés as well as upmarket restaurants, and three locations to go to the movies. The Armitt Collection showcases the work of Kurt Schwitters *(see p40)*, the émigré artist who lived here after the war, as well as delicate watercolours by Beatrix Potter. There is a fine short walk from the heart of the village up the rushing ghyll. It is also a good base for excursions in the Langdale Valley. ✣ *Map F5*

Hardknott Pass

10 Hardknott Pass

You need to brace yourself for the steep zigzag drive over the Hardknott Pass – it is definitely not a good option for fearful drivers. But the views go from impressive to jaw-dropping as you gain in elevation, and the remains of the Roman fort are unmissable, comprising long snaking lines of stone walls. The fort was built during Hadrian's reign, and contained a bath house amongst other buildings, though creature comforts are hard to imagine at this wild, windswept spot. ✣ *Map D6*

A Wordsworthian Walk in the Central Fells

Morning

🕙 Your starting point is **Grasmere**, where the plain graves of Wordsworth, his wife, sister and children can be seen in the graveyard of **St Oswald's Church**. Wander on to **Dove Cottage**, located just east of the village on the main road, where the cottage tour and a visit to the museum will take at least an hour. From here, head up the lane and follow signs for the Coffin Route *(see p8)*, used to carry corpses from Rydal to their resting place in St Oswald's (look out for the stone coffin rests along the way). The walk leads you parallel to the road, but high above it, well away from the traffic.

Afternoon

After around an hour you reach **Rydal**, where the riverside teashop in the grounds of Rydal Hall is a decent spot for lunch. Backtrack slightly to visit Rydal Mount, the poet's home for the last 37 years of his life. Then head down the hill to the church – through the churchyard you reach **Dora's Field** *(see p20)*, planted with daffodils by the Wordsworths when their much loved daughter died in her early 40s. From here, cross over the road, turn right for a few metres and leave the road to cross the little bridge. A path leads you along **Rydal Water**, and then to the foot of Grasmere (lake). You join a lane for the final stretch that circles back to Grasmere village. On the way back into the village, stop at **Faeryland** *(see p61)* on the lake for tea (summer only).

Left **Stickle Ghyll** Centre **Hardknott Pass** Right **Rydal Water**

🔟 Beauty Spots

Skelwith Force
This force lies just west of Skelwith Bridge on the riverside path. Continue past the waterfall and you reach the Cumbria Way route, which winds along the river to Elterwater. ☜ *Map E6*

Dora's Meadow
The field below Rydal Mount was planted with daffodils by Wordsworth and his wife after the death of their daughter Dora. March is the best time to see the flowers in bloom *(see p20)*.

Stickle Ghyll
A very steep and rough walk from the New Dungeon Ghyll Hotel takes you up rushing Stickle Ghyll and up to the high tarn. ☜ *Map E5*

Easedale Tarn
A stiff but wonderful hike from Grasmere leads to Easedale Tarn – one of Wordsworth's favourite spots. ☜ *Map E5*

Loughrigg Tarn
This lovely little body of water sits north of Skelwith Bridge and at the base of Loughrigg Fell, itself considered to have some of the greatest views in the lakes. ☜ *Map E5*

Rydal Water
A scenic path runs south along Rydal Water, connecting Rydal with Grasmere, via the attractive little café and boat hire outfit at Faeryland. ☜ *Map F5*

Helm Crag
The peaks of Helm Crag are called The Lion and The Lamb, for their distinctive shapes. Wainright called it, "an exhilarating little climb, a brief essay in real mountaineering". ☜ *Map E5*

Rydal Hall Grounds
Rydal Hall, opposite Rydal Mount, is a stately Neo-Classical home owned by the diocese of Carlisle. The sweeping grounds are also home to the Full Circle camp site *(see p119)*. ☜ *Map F5*

Hardknott Pass
This hair-raisingly steep road is worth the effort for the views and the substantial and evocative remains of the Hardknott Roman fort. The vista of the fells and the fort are particularly beautiful in the evening light. ☜ *Map D6*

Elterwater
This is a gleaming lake fed by the Brathay, just below the village of Elterwater. Take the path round the lake and on to Ambleside. There is also a bus back to Elterwater. ☜ *Map E5*

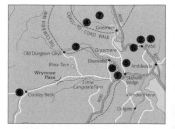

Left **Sign, Wainwright Inn** Centre **Bar, Old Dungeon Ghyll Hotel** Right **Kirkstone Inn**

TOP 10 Pubs and Inns

1 Old Dungeon Ghyll Hotel
A venerable Lakes inn that features the excellent and rugged Hikers Bar, Old Dungeon Ghyll Hotel is propped up by locals and weatherbeaten walkers. There is an outdoor terrace, perfect for a summer pint. ® *Langdale • Map E5 • 015394 37272*

2 New Dungeon Ghyll Hotel
This Victorian hotel to the east of its more famous and older counterpart serves very decent bar meals as well as more upmarket dinners. ® *Great Langdale • Map E5 • 015394 37213*

3 Lamb Inn
A simple and lively pub in the heart of Grasmere, the Lamb Inn is the locals' choice, with a good selection of beers. There is a limited menu of bar meals. ® *Grasmere • Map E5 • 015394 35456*

4 The Unicorn
Tucked away in a steep part of the village, this is a welcoming, old-fashioned pub with live music and a good range of whiskies. ® *North Road, Ambleside • Map F5 • 015394 33216*

5 Wainwrights Inn
A walker's favourite, with hearty helpings of local food such as Cumberland sausage, as well as the requisite flagstoned floors. The inn has a lovely location just outside Chapel Stile. ® *Chapel Stile • Map E5 • 015394 38088*

6 Britannia Inn
One of the most picturesque locations for a Lakes pub, the friendly Britannia Inn sits on Elterwater's village green and is packed with walkers and locals on summer evenings. ® *Elterwater • Map E5 • 015394 37210*

7 Kirkstone Inn
A 500-year-old pub sitting in a truly remote and sometimes cloud-fringed location on the high Kirkstone Pass, with low ceilings, flagstone floors and a timber-framed interior. ® *Kirkstone Pass • Map F5 • 015394 33888*

8 The Traveller's Rest
An ancient inn, sitting on the road that leads north from Grasmere, with cosy rooms for those who want to stay over. It is a good spot for avoiding the crowds in the village itself. ® *North of Grasmere • Map E5 • 015394 35604*

9 Three Shires Inn
This remote old-style inn is a popular stop for walkers in the Langdale Valley, and a jumping-off point for some great hikes. ® *Little Langdale • Map E5 • 015394 37215*

10 The Golden Rule
A good old traditional pub in Ambleside with a fine selection of real ales, a patio garden and strictly no music – it is very popular with locals and walkers. ® *Smithy Brow • Map F5 • 015394 32257*

Left **Shops, Ambleside** Centre **The shop at Dove Cottage** Right **Sarah Nelson's shop**

🔟 Shops and Galleries

1 Sarah Nelson's Gingerbread Shop

Local gingerbread is one of the characteristic tastes and fragrant smells of Grasmere. Baked in the village according to a longheld secret recipe, the gingerbread is sold in this little shop next to St Oswald's Church *(see p8)*.

2 The Shop at Dove Cottage

Everything you have ever wanted to know about the Romantic poets can be found here. There is a full range of poetry titles and biographies, plus notebooks, soaps and other attractive gifts *(see p8)*.

3 Below Stairs

This is a wonderful shop for china, kitchen gadgets, place mats, pepper mills and other hard-to-find kitchenware. 🛇 *Church Street, Ambleside • Map F5 • 015394 34370 • www.below-stairs.co.uk*

4 Outdoor Shops

Ambleside has more outdoor shops than you can believe, so it is a good place to add to your hiking, climbing and mountain-biking kit. You can also pick up local maps and guides here. 🛇 *Ambleside • Map F5*

5 Sam Read's Bookshop

A well-informed owner and a characterful space distinguish this little bookshop in the heart of Grasmere. Its shelves are stacked with local-interest titles, guidebooks, contemporary fiction as well as a strong children's section *(see pp8–9)*.

6 Heaton Cooper Studio

A family-run studio and gallery which sells cards, paintings of the surrounding area, sculpture, and art materials. 🛇 *The Green, Grasmere • Map E5 • 015394 35280 • www.heatoncooper.co.uk*

7 Old Courthouse Gallery

This is one of the largest independent contemporary art galleries in the Lakes, featuring local paintings, crafts, quirky furniture, clocks and handmade glass pieces. 🛇 *Market Place, Ambleside • Map F5 • 015394 32022*

8 The Co-op Village Shop

Founded in the 19th century, this local Co-op is a good place for campers and self-caterers to stock up. They also have a great café. 🛇 *Chapel Stile • Map E5*

9 Lakeland Art Gallery

Around for 30 years, this gallery offers paintings and signed limited edition prints – many are scenes from the Lakes. 🛇 *Grasmere • Map E5 • 015394 35271*

10 Fred Holdsworth's Bookshop

This quaint little store located near the Salutation Hotel in Ambleside is great for maps and guides, as well as a wide range of fiction and history titles. 🛇 *Ambleside • Map F5 • 015394 33388*

Left **Interior of Jumble Room** Centre **Lucy's on a Plate**

🔟 Places to Eat

1 Miller Howe Café
This is the best option for a full English breakfast in Grasmere. It is modern and functional with good service. Internet access provided. ◈ Grasmere • Map E5 • 015394 35234

2 Brambles
Upstairs from the Co-op, Brambles is an attractive and friendly little village café, with a wooden interior, good coffee and excellent home-baked items. ◈ Chapel Stile • Map E5 • 015394 37500

3 Apple Pie Eating House
A bustling café serving good apple pie (as the name suggests) and bath buns. They also let you bring your dog along. ◈ Rydal Road, Ambleside • Map F5 • 015394 33679

4 Rattle Gill Cafe
This cute and friendly café is one of a cluster of attractive white-painted buildings opposite the waterwheel. The cakes are highly recommended. ◈ Ambleside • Map F5 • 015394 31894

5 Lucy's On A Plate
An Ambleside favourite, Lucy's is a cheery café-restaurant serving hearty and filling food. It is busy at all times of day, but looks particularly enticing by candlelight in the evening. There is also a deli counter with freshly baked treats. ◈ Church Street, Ambleside • Map F5• 015394 31191 • £££

6 Jumble Room
A colourful restaurant in Grasmere, with an international menu that includes Italian and Catalan dishes. Closer to home, their fish and chips is also very popular. ◈ Langdale, Grasmere • Map E5 • 015394 35188 • £££

7 Lucy 4
Part of the Lucy's empire, this little wine bar and bistro is decked out in stylish black and red. Mediterranean style mix and match menu. ◈ 2 St Mary's Lane, Ambleside • Map F5 • 015394 34666 • ££

8 Doi Intanon
If you tire of Cumberland sausage, try some flavourful Thai food at this attractive restaurant in central Ambleside. ◈ Market Place, Ambleside • Map F5 • 015394 32119 • ££

9 Zeffirelli's
One of Ambleside's hotspots, Zeffirelli's serves delicious vegetarian mains, pizzas and very large puddings. There is a jazz club upstairs, and a great cinema too. ◈ Compston Road, Ambleside • Map F5 • 015394 33845 • ££

10 Fellini's
A sister restaurant of Zeffirelli's, stylish Fellini's also serves vegetarian food and has a cinema screen, although it is more upmarket. ◈ Church Street, Ambleside • Map F5 • 015394 33845 • ££

Left **Road above Ullswater** Centre **Sleeping Giant, Dalemain** Right **Boats on Ullswater**

Ullswater

Tucked away in the northeast of the region, glacial Ullswater is a wonderfully scenic destination, well geared up for tourists, without being overrun by them. One of the highlights is a pleasurable ride on the historic steamboat, which will take you from Glenridding in the south via Howtown to attractive Pooley Bridge in the northeast. This area is renowned for its majestic scenery. Glenridding is the starting point for hikes up Helvellyn, while a less ambitious walk takes you to the gushing falls of Aira Force.

Gillside camp site, Glenridding

🔟 Sights

1. Ullswater Steamer
2. Glenridding
3. Aira Force
4. Dacre
5. Dalemain
6. Patterdale
7. Helvellyn
8. Lowther Park
9. Pooley Bridge
10. Howtown

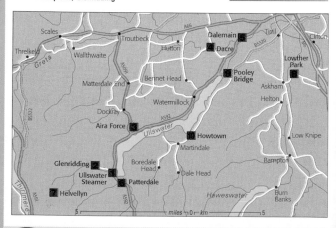

1 Ullswater Steamer

Long and elegant, the red-funnelled Victorian steamers are a fine sight on Ullswater, ferrying passengers up and down the lake from Glenridding to Pooley Bridge, with a stop half-way at Howtown. Head to the pier at Glenridding to find out more about tickets, timings and special cruises, such as the bird-watching trip and the *ceilidh* (Gaelic dancing) cruise. There is a café at the pier, and the boats are equipped with bars.
◈ *Glenridding • Map F4 • 017684 82229 • Daily • Adm • www.ullswater-steamers.co.uk*

2 Glenridding

Extending from the shores of Ullswater up the steep sides of the fells, Glenridding is a pleasing little village. There are no great sights but that is compensated by a lively holiday atmosphere. Some old-fashioned village shops, outdoor stores and a few cafés and pubs are sustained by the hordes of walkers who come here in all weathers to tackle nearby Helvellyn. Outdoor types head up to the remote Helvellyn hostel, or pitch up at idyllic Gillside camp site. There are many easier treks for less intrepid walkers. ◈ *Map F4*

Aira Force

3 Aira Force

There are plenty of walks to forces in the Lakes, but this is one of the most satisfying. Aira Force, 20 m (66 ft), is framed by two stone bridges. William and Dorothy Wordsworth visited the surrounding hills in 1802 and it was her diary entry describing the daffodils that prompted one of the most famous poems in the English language. The foot-paths continue beyond the waterfall to Dockray. ◈ *Map F4*

4 Dacre

Attractive Dacre village is home to romantic 13th-century Dacre Castle. Nearby is a restored Norman church, St Andrew's: fragments of Viking crosses can be seen in the chancel, and in the graveyard sit four stone effigies, known as the Dacre bears. The Horse and Farrier pub *(see p86)*, completes the picture. ◈ *Map G3*

Glenridding, viewed from Gillside

Georgian picture gallery, Dalemain

The Vikings in Ullswater

There is evidence for Viking settlement at Ullswater in the very name of the lake – it is thought to have been named for a chieftain, Ulf, who ruled the area 1,200 years ago. An alternative suggestion is that it was named in honour of the Viking God Ullr. Earthworks on the north shore are said to conceal the remains of a Viking settlement.

Dalemain

Like many of the Lake District houses, Dalemain has been in the same family for a very long time – more than 300 years in this case. An elegant pink-hued Georgian façade conceals the building's real age: it was built around a 12th-century defensive tower, and is mainly Elizabethan. In addition to the panelled interiors and family portraits, there is a good café in the medieval hall. The children's garden with its adorable sleeping giant should not be missed.
❂ Map G3 • 017684 86450 • Open Easter–Oct: 11:15am–4pm Sun–Thu, Oct: 11:15am–3pm • Adm • www. dalemain.com

Patterdale

Patterdale (named for St Patrick) is another pleasant and low-key little settlement that sits in a cluster on the road to Glenridding. The village is a starting point for a number of walks. There are a couple of pubs here, notably the walkers' favourite the White Lion, plus a good chalet-style youth hostel, and a waterside camp site: Side Farm. This is worth a visit for non-campers too as there is a great little teashop in the farmyard, located beside an 18th-century barn (see p87). ❂ Map F4

Helvellyn

The third-highest mountain in England, Helvellyn is quite popular. The narrow Striding Edge ascent is just as edgy as it sounds, and involves a scramble to the summit. There are plenty of other approaches that are less perilous, but whichever route you go for do not ascend Helvellyn unless you are well-equipped and reasonably fit. Detailed advice on routes and weather conditions can be obtained at the tourist information centre at Glenridding. ❂ Map E4

Lowther Park

This is the estate of a ruined Victorian-Gothic castle – an imposing structure whose sorry state lends the surrounding parkland an air of melancholy. Two of the estate villages are lined with more cheerful painted Georgian houses and there is an

Patterdale village

Bird of Prey Centre, Lowther Park

interesting if slightly bizarre attraction in the form of the Bird of Prey Centre, where you can watch kestrels and falcons being put through their paces. A farm building here has been converted into a very pleasant tea shop.
⊗ Map G3 • Bird of Prey Centre; 01931 712746; Open Apr–Oct: 11am–5pm; flying demonstrations: 2–4pm

Pooley Bridge

Built around its high-arched stone bridge, Pooley Bridge is a handsome lakeside village that becomes rather traffic-heavy at busy times, as it is a stop on the steamer route. Nonetheless it is worth a visit for the market that is open on the last Sunday of the month from April to September. This is a good resource if you are self-catering, with a variety of local produce on offer. The best pub in the village is the 18th-century Sun Inn, which sits near the main square (see p86). ⊗ Map G3

Howtown

The Ullswater Steamer drops many walkers at Howtown, which is little more than a row of houses and the Howtown Hotel. Above the village, follow the road uphill to lovely St Martin's, a plain Elizabethan church embraced by a yew tree. To walk to Patterdale, either follow the lakeshore route or head through the Boredale valley, with a dramatic ascent and descent at the end of the walk. ⊗ Map G4

A Day in Ullswater

Morning

Starting from **Glenridding**, take the bus along the western side of the lake (this is not a particularly pleasant walk due to traffic on the lake road). After a couple of miles, get off the bus for the signposted walk up to **Aira Force**. This walk takes around 40 minutes there and back, although the path continues uphill to the village of Dockray if you want to carry on. You can have morning coffee at the basic but decent **Aira Force Tearoom** (see p87) at the beginning of the walk. Get back on the bus, and carry on up the northern shore to **Pooley Bridge**, where you can relax over a pint at the **Sun Inn** or the **Pooley Bridge Inn** (see p86).

Afternoon

From Pooley Bridge, take the historic steamer down the lake. You could choose to return directly to Glenridding, or disembark at Howtown. From here, follow the lane uphill to **St Martin's Church**. Either retrace your steps to the ferry or – if you have the time, energy and an OS map, follow the track and footpath for the wonderful hike to **Patterdale** before making your way back to Glenridding. You have a choice of two very distinct walking routes – the low-level option takes you along the lakeshore to Patterdale, while the route through the Boredale Valley involves a steep climb to ascend the valley wall, from where you dip down into the village – a gorgeous sight in the evening light.

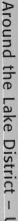

Left **Traveller's Rest** Right **White Lion**

Pubs and Inns

1 Traveller's Rest
Head up the hill in the village to reach this ancient inn, the best in the area. There is a terrace for the summer months, and it is often packed with walkers. *Glenridding • Map F4 • 017684 82298*

2 Horse and Farrier
Tucked away in one of the quietest and prettiest villages in the Ullswater area, this venerable 18th-century pub makes a perfect stop for a pint. The outdoor seating and the wholesome food are a bonus. *Dacre • Map G3 • 017684 86541*

3 White Lion
Good food and real ales are served in this classic and convivial village inn. The food, which is above-average pub grub, really hits the spot if you have been on a long walk. *Patterdale • Map F4 • 017684 82214*

4 The Patterdale Hotel
The hotel's Place Fell Inn is nice for an alfresco drink; the beer garden is a lush spot to relax in the summer sun with a pint of ale. *Patterdale • Map F4 • 017684 82231*

5 Brackenrigg Inn
This traditional wayside inn at the northeastern shore of the lake has a basic, WiFi enabled bar, as well as a more upmarket dining room and lovely views from the terrace. *Ullswater • Map G3 • 017684 86206*

6 Pooley Bridge Inn
An unusual balconied building, this inn is in the centre of Pooley Bridge. It is wreathed with hanging baskets in summer; inside, there is a timber ceiling and fires if it is cold. *Pooley Bridge • Map G3 • 017684 86215*

7 Brotherswater Inn
This wayside inn sits right on the roadside, near the Kirkstone Pass on the way to Ullswater. It is very popular with ale-drinking hikers. *Brotherswater • Map F4 • 017684 82239*

8 The Quiet Bar
This quirky camp site bar was converted from an ancient barn in the 1950s. It is worth spending a night in a tent to sample the "Quiet Pint" – the camp site's own brew. *Quiet Site camping, Ullswater • Map F3 • 07768 727016*

9 Sun Inn
Housed in an ivy-covered building, which was converted from a row of ancient cottages, the Sun Inn serves Jennings Ales, including the bizarrely named Cock-a-Hoop and Sneck-Lifter. *Pooley Bridge • Map G3 • 017684 86205*

10 The Ramblers Bar
The bar is located in an annexe to the Inn on the Lake hotel, prettily placed on the Ullswater shore. There is real ale, large pub meals and snooker. *Inn on the Lake, Glenridding • Map F4 • 017684 82444*

Price Categories

For a three-course meal for one with half a bottle of wine (or equivalent meal), taxes and extra charges.

£	under £25
££	£25–£35
£££	£35–£50
££££	over £50

Left **Dalemain Tearoom** Centre **Exterior of Fellbites**

🔟 Places to Eat

1 Sharrow Bay Hotel
Enjoy Michelin-starred food in this plush hotel on the eastern side of the lake. Dress up, take your credit card and enjoy a bird's eye view of the water lapping below. ⊗ *Map G4 • 01768 486301 • ££££*

2 Greystones
Brightly painted and cheery Greystones café serves soups, sandwiches and cakes, and sits by the beck in Glenridding. They also have WiFi – something of a rarity in these parts. ⊗ *Glenridding • Map F4 • 017684 82392*

3 Dalemain Tearoom
Try the tea and cakes in a rugged medieval hall that is part of Dalemain's wonderful miscellany of historic buildings; they also offer light lunches and sell country-house produce to take away. ⊗ *Dalemain House • Map G3 • 017684 86450 • Open Easter–Oct*

4 Greystoke Cycle Café
A great little stop for long-distance cyclists, this lakeland farmhouse has all kinds of bicycle paraphernalia. There is also a café and tea-garden dishing up pastas, bacon sandwiches and cakes. ⊗ *Greystoke • Map G2 • 017684 83984 • Open for cyclists: daily; general public: Fri & Sat*

5 Inn on the Lake
This lakeside hotel is a convenient stop for afternoon tea; you can enjoy the view across the lake from the terrace or lounge while tucking into the tasty traditional fare made from local produce. ⊗ *Glenridding • Map F4 • 017684 82444*

6 Treetops
Treetops café is a reliable stop for coffee or a light lunch in the centre of Pooley Bridge; they have a few outdoor seats. ⊗ *Pooley Bridge • Map G3 • 017684 8626*

7 Fellbites
A handsome ochre-coloured house, Fellbites serves hearty, reasonably priced dishes such as Welsh rarebit. The little patch of garden is a good suntrap. ⊗ *Glenridding • Map F4 • 017684 82781*

8 Granny Dowbekin's
The garden at Granny Dowbekin's offers the best view of Pooley Bridge. The tearoom specializes in all-day breakfasts, featuring fresh bakes. ⊗ *Pooley Bridge • Map G3 • 017684 86453*

9 Aira Force Tearooms
Very handy for a pre- or post-walk cup. Good spicy soups and sandwiches are provided by a local hotel. ⊗ *At the foot of Aira Force • Map F4 • 017684 82881*

10 Side Farm Tearoom
Homebaking, hot drinks, and ice creams are served in the tearoom in a yard at Side Farm camp site. ⊗ *Side Farm camping, near Patterdale • Map F4 • 077961 28897*

Left **Georgian houses, Cockermouth** Centre **Laurel and Hardy's car, Keswick** Right **Mirehouse**

The Northwest

THE NORTHWEST OF THE REGION *has plenty of contrasts – Borrowdale is one of the most verdant valleys in the Lakes, with lofty mountains and enticing hamlets, while at Honister the scenery is at its starkest and most forbidding. There is a welcoming stately home at Mirehouse, on the shores of Bassenthwaite, while to the west are deprived coastal towns such as Workington. Just outside the national park sits Cockermouth, a handsome Georgian settlement most famous for the National Trust-owned Wordsworth House. The town was severely battered by the floods of 2009, and the recovery is determined but necessarily slow.*

All Saint's Church, Cockermouth

Castlerigg Stone Circle

Sights

1. Cockermouth
2. Mirehouse
3. Buttermere
4. Grange-in-Borrowdale
5. Derwent Water
6. Keswick
7. Honister Pass
8. Castlerigg Stone Circle
9. Haystacks
10. Cat Bells

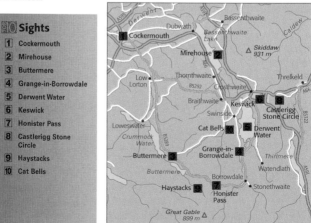

Preceding pages **Castlerigg Stone Circle**

Bridge Inn, Buttermere

Cockermouth

With its brightly painted Georgian houses and grand main street, Cockermouth feels very different from the grey-stone settlements of the national park. It was pounded by the floods in 2009; the main street turned into a torrent, with whole trees being swept down it. The remarkable Wordsworth House survived relatively unscathed due to its height, but many shops and businesses were destroyed, meaning this attractive town is sadly slow on the road to recovery. ✆ Map C2

Mirehouse

This stately home of the Spedding family, built in the mid-17th century, is one of the most inviting in the Lakes. There are display cases featuring correspondence between past Speddings and Thomas Carlyle, Constable, Tennyson and Wordsworth. What distinguishes the house is its serenity and light-filled rooms, and the thought that's gone into making it an attraction for kids with its family nature trail and four play areas. ✆ 5 km (3 miles) north of Keswick • Map D2 • 017687 72287 • House: open Apr–Oct 2–5pm Wed & Sun; Garden: open Mar–Oct 10am–5pm daily • Adm • www. mirehouse.com

Buttermere

Tiny Buttermere is a beautifully sited and attractive Lakes village, with high peaks looming above in all directions. It is a haven for walkers, many of whom tackle Haystacks from here; early starts, long hikes and restorative pints at the two excellent pubs here are the order of the day. Otherwise, there is a YHA hostel, rooms at the pubs, a camp site with an idyllic setting, and home-made ice cream from Syke Farm (see p97). ✆ Map C4

Grange-in-Borrowdale

The village of Grange is the gateway to lush Borrowdale, sitting at the valley's northern end. Reached over an old stone bridge, it is an ideal place to rest after a walk on a summer's day. You can get tea and cake from the teashop, and sit in the garden by the river, watching people amble in over the bridge. A low-key but lovely attraction. ✆ Map D4

Grange-in-Borrowdale

Derwent Water

Derwent Water

Derwent Water is one of the loveliest lakes, and one of the easiest to explore by boat. The Keswick Launch makes regular circuits from Keswick itself, with six stops at regular intervals around the lakeshore. This means that the fells that ring the lake are very easy to access without the hassle of driving – you can easily reach Walla Crag and Cat Bells for example. The lake is also great for watersports, from a gentle paddle in a canoe to windsurfing – try Derwent Water Marina at Portinscale for boat hire and instructions. ✎ *Map D3*
• *Derwent Water Marina: 017687 72912; www.derwentwatermarina.co.uk*

Keswick

If you have had a couple of days of walking in the wilds, the town of Keswick will feel downright cosmopolitan – there is a cinema, a theatre, a handful of museums, pubs that get packed out at weekends with walkers and locals and a number of decent restaurants and cafés. It does not have the charm of Ambleside or Grasmere, but there is some fine Victorian architecture, and the expansive lakefront, lined with long wooden rowing boats, is very attractive on a summer evening *(see pp28–9)*.

The 2009 Floods

In November 2009, west Cumbria suffered perhaps the most severe flooding in a thousand years. The worst-hit town was Cockermouth, with the rescue services receiving praise for their rescue of 200 people from their homes as the waters rose. In northern Workington, a policeman was killed when a bridge collapsed as he was directing drivers to safety.

Honister Pass

From Buttermere, the narrow road snakes up steep inclines, stark fells rising high on either side, to the final push that takes you to the Honister Slate Mine. This is still a working mine, but it is also a museum and a memorial to the miners who lived and worked and died here in centuries past. Underground tours relate how children as young as 8 worked here, in appalling conditions. On a lighter note, there is a shop selling slate paraphernalia *(see p95)*. Beyond the mine, the road slopes down to the alluring environs of Borrowdale. ✎ *Map D4*

Castlerigg Stone Circle

Close to Keswick, enjoying a gloriously open panoramic backdrop, the Castlerigg Stone Circle is one of the most lovely and theatrical in the country. Comprising 38 stones, it is

Museum in Keswick

thought to have been created around 3000 BC. As with all such ancient structures, including Stonehenge, its exact purpose is something of a mystery, though it may have had an astronomical purpose. ◈ *Map E3*

Haystacks
From Buttermere village, many walkers make the iconic 13-km (8-mile) hike to Haystacks, which was Alfred Wainwright's favourite peak, via Red Pike, High Stile and High Crag. The summit is dotted with tarns, including Innominate Tarn. Here Wainwright's ashes were scattered, as he requested, writing: "if you, dear reader, should get a bit of grit in your boot as you are crossing Haystacks… please treat it with respect. It might be me". ◈ *Map D4*

Cat Bells

Cat Bells
From Hawes End pier on Derwent Water, the path to Cat Bells path climbs steeply to 1,481 ft (452 m); the name stems from a Norse belief that the hill was home to a den of wildcats. It is a steep hike, but one that will reward you with a sweeping panorama of the lake on a clear day. Descending from Cat Bells, you could head to the Swinside Inn, a mile from Hawes End. ◈ *Map D4*

A Drive in the Northwest Lakes

Morning

From **Keswick**, drive west on the B5292, over the **Whinlatter Pass**. Then take the road south and stop at the idyllic village of **Buttermere**, which sits under a line of mountains: take a look at the church of St James, and maybe indulge in a home-made ice cream from Syke Farm. From here the road climbs steeply, culminating in the jagged **Honister Pass**. At the top of the pass you can stop at the **Honister Slate Mine** *(see p95)*, either to buy a slate souvenir, or to take a mine tour (10:30am, 12:30pm, 2pm and 3:30pm). The pass then drops into the greener and more welcoming environment of **Borrowdale**. The first stop is the rugged but pretty village of **Seatoller**, where the Yew Tree café is an excellent refreshment stop.

Afternoon

From here, you can potter through the Borrowdale valley, perhaps with a detour to **Stonethwaite** and a stop at **Rosthwaite** *(see p94)* – both are beautiful hamlets with whitewashed buildings. From Rosthwaite you could stretch your legs with the pleasant footpath walk up to **Castle Crag** *(see p94)*. Further on, make a stop at the National Trust for the short walk to the **Bowderstone** *(see p94)*, a huge boulder which can be accessed by a wooden ladder. And then cross the river to the idyllic Grange for a cup of tea and a scone by the river. Drive back to Keswick up the eastern shore of the lake – altogether less hair-raising than the Honister Pass.

Left **Walk to Castle Crag** Centre **Seatoller** Right **Interior of Mirehouse, Bassenthwaite**

🔟 Best of the Rest

Stonethwaite
An ancient settlement in the heart of Borrowdale, this small village is home to the renowned Langstrath Country Inn, named for the looming valley that lies just beyond the village. 🗺 Map D4

Thornthwaite, Whinlatter
An attractive little place with good local walks and an excellent gallery and tearoom, which is a great place to buy local arts and crafts. 🗺 Map D3

Whinlatter Forest Park
This mountainous forest is a great place to go for spectacular views of the Lake District, nature-spotting, mountain biking and walking trails. 🗺 West of Keswick • Map D3 • Visitors' Centre open Apr–Oct: 10am–5pm daily; Nov–Mar: 10am–4pm daily; closed Jan • 017687 78469 • www.visitlakelandforests.co.uk

Castle Crag
A distinctive landmark in Borrowdale, Castle Crag is perfect if you fancy a relatively short but satisfying walk. 🗺 Map D4

Seatoller
A welcoming little white-washed hamlet at the foot of the Honister Pass, Seatoller is home to one of the area's best and quirkiest cafés: the Yew Tree (see p97). 🗺 Map D4

Caldbeck
This gorgeous village was once home to a number of mills. However, Caldbeck is most famous for the elaborate tomb of legendary local hunter John Peel. 🗺 Map E1

Seathwaite
Sitting at the end of the road, this tiny place gets deluged with visitors as it is the starting point for the hikes to Scafell Pike and Great Gable. 🗺 Map D4

Bowderstone
One of the region's odder attractions – a gigantic and photogenic boulder brought here from Scotland by a glacier. A ladder takes you to the top. 🗺 Map D4

Rosthwaite
An archetypal Borrowdale hamlet with whitewashed houses and an excellent local café, the Flock-In (see p97). 🗺 Map D4

Bassenthwaite
The highlights of this less-travelled lake include the house and gardens of Mirehouse (see p91) as well as rich birdlife including ospreys. 🗺 Map D2

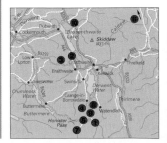

Left **Pottery, Northern Lights Gallery** Centre **Castlegate House Gallery** Right **George Fisher**

⟨TOP⟩10 Shops and Galleries

1 Northern Lights Gallery
A smart commercial gallery that sells black and white photographic prints, watercolour and oil paintings, drawings, sculpture, jewellery and local pottery. ⟨◈⟩ *22 St Johns Street, Keswick • Map T5 • 017687 75402 • www. northernlightsgallery.co.uk*

2 Castlegate House Gallery
This lovely, light- and art-filled house comprises the best commercial gallery in the Lakes. They focus on British art, and the garden is dotted with sculptures *(see p34)*.

3 Keswick Brewing Company
Take a tour of the brewery and then buy a few bottles of their "Thirst" ales – all with bold and distinctive labels. Booking is essential. ⟨◈⟩ *The Old Brewery, Brewery Lane, Keswick • Map T4 • 017687 80700 • www.keswickbrewery.co.uk*

4 Honister Slate Mine shop
All sorts of slate items are available at the mine shop, including birdbaths, statuary, place mats and made-to-order signs for your house. ⟨◈⟩ *Honister Slate Mine • Map D4 • 017687 77230 • www.honistergreenslate.com*

5 Pencil Museum Shop
A treasure trove for budding artists, where you can buy any type or colour of pencil. ⟨◈⟩ *Southby Works, Keswick • Map S4 • 017687 73626 • www.percyhouse.co.uk*

6 Sharp Edge Gallery
Located by the River Greta near the Pencil Museum, this little gallery is another good outlet for local arts and crafts. ⟨◈⟩ *135 Main Street, Keswick • Map S4 • 017687 73788*

7 Bitter Beck Pottery
Displays the ceramics and stoneware of Joan Hardie, whose work is inspired by the natural forms of leaves, bark and lichen. ⟨◈⟩ *11 Market Place, Cockermouth • Map C2 • 07803 174120 • www. bitterbeck.oo.uk*

8 Thornthwaite Galleries
A respected gallery outside Keswick that sells paintings, sculpture, jewellery and pottery; there is also a tea shop. ⟨◈⟩ *Thornthwaite • Map D3 • 017687 78248 • www.thornthwaitegalleries.co.uk*

9 George Fisher Outdoor Shop
Set in a magnificent stone building, George Fisher's has everything required for an outdoor trip, plus expert advice from knowledgeable staff. ⟨◈⟩ *2 Borrowdale Road, Keswick • Map T5 • 017687 72178*

10 Viewpoints Gallery
This gallery features local photographer Pete Tasker's impressive pictures of the lakes, tarns and ghylls. They stock large format prints and greeting cards. ⟨◈⟩ *St Johns Street Keswick • Map T5 • 017687 74449 • www.petetasker.co.uk*

Left **Langstrath Country Inn** Centre **Dog & Gun** Right **The Fish Inn**

TOP 10 Pubs and Inns

1 Bitter End
A handsome, old-fashioned, cream-painted pub and restaurant, Bitter End has its own micro-brewery. In December the Cockermouth Beer Festival is held at the nearby Kirkgate Centre. ✆ 15 Kirkgate, Cockermouth • Map C2 • 01900 828993

2 Dog & Gun
Located in the heart of Keswick, the traditional Dog & Gun gets packed on Saturdays after the market, and the real ales make it a magnet for walkers year-round. ✆ 2 Lake Road, Keswick • Map T5 • 017687 73463

3 Royal Oak
A family-run hotel in the hamlet of Borrowdale. There is a snug bar serving local beers and a lovely open fire. ✆ Rosthwaite • Map D4 • 017687 77214

4 Kirkstile Inn
This 400-year-old inn, located between Loweswater and Crummock Water, has open fires and a wealth of history. The inn serves upmarket dinners and also provides accommodation. ✆ Loweswater • Map C3 • 01900 85219

5 The Pheasant Inn
Worth a peek to feel the atmosphere of a very ancient traditional English wayside inn – this place is 500 years old, with log fires, low beams and narrow corridors. ✆ Bassenthwaite • Map D2 • 017687 76234

6 Bank Tavern
Cask ales and decent pub meals are on offer at this pub in central Keswick. It has a beer garden, and the decor, though plain, is attractive. ✆ 47 Main Street, Keswick • Map T5 • 017687 72663

7 The Bridge
This fine stone building sits by the bridge in Buttermere; at the Walker's Bar you can have a pint of Black Sheep and sample Cumbrian pub grub. ✆ Buttermere • Map C4 • 017687 70252

8 The Fish Inn
A whitewashed hotel in a remote and enticing Lakes village. Mary Robinson, the one-time barmaid and famous beauty, known as the Maid of Buttermere, drew visitors from miles around – even Wordsworth came to see her. ✆ Buttermere • Map C4 • 017687 70253

9 The Wheatsheaf Inn
A Jennings pub, the 17th-century Wheatsheaf Inn has everything you'd want in a country pub: beer garden, open fire, real ales and pub grub, as well as fancier food. ✆ Low Lorton • Map C3 • 01900 85199

10 Langstrath Country Inn
This family-run inn in the unspoilt village of Stonethwaite started as a miner's cottage in the late-16th century. It is very popular with walkers. ✆ Stonethwaite • Map D4 • 017687 77239

Left **Quince & Medlar** Centre **Lakeland Pedlar** Right **The Old Sawmill Tearoom**

🔟 Restaurants and Cafés

Yew Tree
This characterful café in the heart of pretty Seatoller features climbing-related memorabilia and pictures and home-baked cakes, in addition to a well-stocked bar.
Ⓢ Seatoller • Map D4

Quince & Medlar
A lovely wood-panelled dining room where inventive vegetarian food and organic wines are served – it's one of the best in the northwest.
Ⓢ 13 Castlegate, Cockermouth
• Map C2 • 01900 823579 • ££

Syke Farm Café
At Syke Farm's Café, they serve ice cream created with milk from their own Ayrshire cows. The more challenging options include bubble gum and liquorice, plus there's excellent lemon meringue pie. Ⓢ Buttermere
• Map C4

Grange Bridge Tearoom
A simple but pleasant little place that has a very attractive garden looking out at the river. They serve soup, sandwiches, tea, coffee and cakes. Ⓢ Grange-in-Borrowdale • Map D4

Lakeland Pedlar
Fresh, home-made vegetarian food, with good breakfasts, and substantial mains and salads for lunch. Decorated with cycling-related posters and memorabilia; there's a bike shop upstairs. Ⓢ Bell Close, Keswick • Map T5 • 017687 74492

Merienda
This relaxed and stylish café and bar serves tapas, alongside a range of Fairtrade foods. There is live music on Fridays.
Ⓢ 7a Station Street, Cockermouth
• Map C2 • 01900 822790

Good Taste
Deli sandwiches, excellent salads, soups, smoothies, brownies, muffins and melts are served at this smart little daytime café in the middle of Keswick. Ⓢ 19 Lake Road, Keswick
• Map T5 • 017687 75973

The Old Sawmill Tearoom
Opposite the entrance to Mirehouse there is a simple stone building housing the basic but reliably good Old Sawmill Tearoom. From here, walks radiate in all directions. Ⓢ Mirehouse, Bassenthwaite Lake • Map D2

The Flock-In
With its punning menu and delightful rustic environs, the Flock-In is a gem of a tearoom. They serve Herdwick stew with home-made scones, pasties and even sell grey Herdwick wool blankets. Ⓢ Rosthwaite • Map D4
• 017687 77675

Armathwaite Hall
A wonderful fine dining experience provided by one of the region's top hotels. Seasonal produce is used and the influence is French and English. Ⓢ Bassenthwaite
• Map D2 • 017687 76551 • £££

For a guide to restaurant prices **See p71.**

Left **Castle, Egremont** Centre **Gosforth** Right **Bridge Inn, Santon Bridge**

Whitehaven and Wasdale

THIS RELATIVELY SMALL AREA PACKS IN A LOT *in terms of history and geography, taking you from the once-grand town of Whitehaven, whose buildings reflect the riches harvested during the slave trade, to the increasingly narrow and remote road that runs from the village of Gosforth into the majestic Wasdale Valley, a magnet for walkers and adventure-sport enthusiasts. The coast hereabouts is rather sullied by the major road that runs along it, but if you hit some good weather you might want to head to St Bees for a swim. Otherwise, go inland for some truly great outdoors.*

Wild Ennerdale

Sights

1. Wasdale Head
2. Gosforth
3. Great Gable
4. St Bees Head
5. Whitehaven
6. Nether Wasdale
7. Ennerdale
8. Egremont
9. Wast Water
10. Santon Bridge

1 Wasdale Head

Fabled for its views and for its role in the development of climbing, Wasdale Head has been on the map for serious hikers for more than a hundred years. The churchyard of tiny St Olaf's, one of the few buildings at the valley head, is scattered with the graves of young men who died in early ascents of the peaks here. There is a renowned hotel and pub, a camping shop, and a couple of camp sites and, of course, the panorama of epic mountains *(see p26).*

Ritson's Bar, Wasdale Head

2 Gosforth

The little village of Gosforth is a handy stop for campers on the way to Wasdale as it has a grocery store and a bakery – as well as a café and a couple of pubs. The must-see sight is located in the graveyard of St Mary's Church: an immensely tall and slender Viking Cross which depicts the victory of Christianity over paganism. Inside the church are two "hogback" Viking tombs. ◈ *Map B6*

3 Great Gable

Pyramidal Great Gable is very easily identifiable from Wasdale Head. If you set your sights on climbing it, then be sure to check the weather first and leave plenty of time for the 2,700-ft (840-m) climb. The beginning of the route, along the valley floor, is interesting – take time to visit the plain little church of St Olaf's, whose beams were made from Viking longships, and note the thick stone walls throughout the valley that were built in the 18th and 19th centuries to pasture sheep. ◈ *Map A5*

4 St Bees Head

There is a substantial stretch of sand beach at St Bees Head, nicely framed by red sandstone cliffs colonized by wonderful birds including guillemot, puffins and razorbills. The beach itself is a Site of Special Scientific interest due to the varieties of crab, mussels and shellfish that inhabit it, although most visitors, especially children, will be more interested in the ice cream van in the car park and a paddle in the sea. ◈ *Map D5*

St Bees Head

Around the Lake District – Whitehaven and Wasdale

Rum Story in Whitehaven

Whitehaven
5 The coastal town of Whitehaven was once the third-largest port in Britain: it grew rich on the export of coal and the import of rum and tobacco. The Georgian townscape reflects this former glory. While it is evident that the town has fallen on harder times, there have been efforts to re-energize and develop the harbour for recreation, and it certainly makes an interesting stop-off for a couple of hours. ◈ Map A4

Nether Wasdale
6 This is one of the prettiest villages in the area, with an open and inviting aspect: two good pubs, the Screes Inn and the Strands Hotel, face each other over the manicured village green. Both pubs provide good accommodation and food and there is a youth hostel nearby, so it is a good base for the gentler walks than those on offer at Wasdale, plus you can access Eskdale easily from here. ◈ Map C5

Ennerdale
7 Ennerdale, the lush and lonely valley to Wasdale's north, is the site of a new development in the Lakes: it has been styled "Wild Ennerdale" by a group that includes the Forestry Commission. The plan is to allow no human intervention, but to observe what occurs in the valley when nature has its way. However, recreation is encouraged: you can cycle or horse-ride along the forest roads, climb Pillar Rock, or walk along Ennerdale Water, fringed by high mountains. ◈ Map B4 • www.wildennerdale.co.uk

Egremont
8 There are two reasons to visit Egremont: one is to see the red sandstone remains of

Nether Wasdale

the Norman castle, itself built on the site of a Danish fort. The other is the Egremont Crab Fair, held in September, which has been running since 1267. This is in fact nothing to do with crabs, but refers to the feudal tradition of handing out crab apples to the peasantry. The main events now are the World Gurning (face-pulling) Championships, Cumberland Wrestling and the singing of hunting songs *(see p43)*. ✎ Map B5

Reflected mountains, Wast Water

Wast Water
Wast Water sits alongside the road into Wasdale valley, backed by forbidding scree-covered slopes: at 5 km (3 miles) long and with a depth of 79 m (260 ft), it is an impressive sight in itself. At the far end of the lake there is a National Trust camp site, which makes a good base for exploration hereabouts. Wordsworth described the lake as, "long, narrow, stern and desolate". ✎ Map C5

Santon Bridge
Santon Bridge, which is located between Wasdale and Eskdale, is another pretty little place, with the River Irt flowing through it. You can camp on the lush lawns of The Old Post Office camp site on the banks of the river. The village's main claim to fame though is The Santon Bridge Inn, world-famous for the long-running Biggest Liar in the World Competition *(see p43)*. ✎ Map C6

A Drive from Whitehaven to Wasdale

Morning

Start your day in **Whitehaven**, with time to visit the harbour and soak up some of the town's history, either at the **Beacon** or at the **Rum Story Museum**. There are a handful of cafés for a morning coffee, the one at the base of the Beacon being probably the most appealing. From here, take the coastal road (which runs parallel to the A595) south, pausing at **St Bees** to look at the priory there. Return to the A595, and continue to the village of **Gosforth**, with a stop-off to see the tall Viking Cross in the churchyard. Then head west on the minor road to **Nether Wasdale**, where the **Screes Inn** *(see p103)* is an excellent lunch stop.

Afternoon

On a clear day, from here the narrow road takes you on the panoramic drive along **Wast Water**, backed by scree that is often reflected in the still water. At the road's end you come to the famously spectacular **Wasdale Head**, where the valley is perfect for some gentle exploration on foot. You can visit the tiny church of **St Olaf's**, or simply walk through the valley along the high stone walls and soak in the mountain views. Dinner is provided at the **Wasdale Head Inn** *(see p103)*, or there is great bar food at the adjoining **Ritson's Bar**. Hole up either at the inn, or at the basic camp site nearby or the better equipped National Trust site. Then you are all set to tackle a mountain the following day: Great Gable is fairly easy to access from here, with panoramic views.

Left **The Beacon** Centre **St Olaf's Church** Right **Wild Ennerdale**

Best of the Rest

1 St Olaf's Church
Mostly rebuilt in the 19th-century, tiny St Olaf's is one of the handful of buildings at Wasdale Head *(see p27)*.

2 The Beacon
This striking building resembles a lighthouse and houses a museum with interactive exhibits. ✪ *Whitehaven • Map A4 • 01946 592302 • 10am–4:30pm Tue–Sun • Adm • www.thebeacon-whitehaven.co.uk*

3 Crow's Nest, Whitehaven
A tall, modern tower by the sea, the Crow's Nest is lit up at night. It is a landmark location during the town's annual maritime festival. ✪ *Whitehaven • Map A4*

4 St Nicholas Church
The ruins of this old Victorian church have been restored and wreathed with plants and flowers. It forms the centrepiece of a pretty park in the middle of the town. ✪ *Whitehaven • Map A4*

5 Calder Bridge
Despite being located near the nuclear facility at Sellafield, little Calder Bridge is worth a visit for a stroll to the ruins of a 12th-century abbey. ✪ *Map B5*

6 Coast-to-Coast Walk, St Bees
Devised by Alfred Wainwright, this long-distance walk takes you from St Bees in the west to Robin's Hood Bay in the east. ✪ *Map A5 • www.coast2coast.co.uk*

7 The Rum Story
Located in an 18th-century warehouse, this is a good attraction for kids, with plenty of lively tableaux recreating the history of Whitehaven and its connection with the Americas. ✪ *Lowther Street, Whitehaven • Map A4 • 01946 592 933 • www.rumstory.co.uk*

8 St Bees
This small attractive village on the route to the sea at St Bees Head has a couple of pubs. Its main draw is the 12th-century priory. ✪ *Map A5*

9 Ennerdale Bridge
Sitting on the route of the Coast-to-Coast Walk, Ennerdale Bridge is visited by walkers, who cluster in the Shepherd's Arms pub. This village is the gateway for visiting Wild Ennerdale. ✪ *Map B4*

10 Black Sail YHA
If you want to get away from it all, hike through Ennerdale to the YHA's most remote hostel, a mountain bothy (hut) at the head of the valley. ✪ *Map C4 • 0845 371 9680 • www.yha.org.uk*

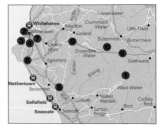

Left **Ritson's Bar** Centre **Interior, Wasdale Head Inn** Right **The Screes Inn sign**

TOP 10 Cafés, Restaurants and Pubs

Wasdale Head Inn
The dining room at the inn is oak-panelled and elegant, with black and white photos of old climbers on the walls. The food is good, with Herdwick lamb much in evidence in season. § *Wasdale Head • Map D5 • 019467 26229 • ££*

Bridge Inn
This famous inn, which hosts the World's Biggest Liar Competition *(see p43)*, is worth a visit at any time for the beer, the food and the warm welcome. § *Santon Bridge • Map C6 • 019467 26221*

The Strands Inn
A handsome village inn with a good reputation for its locally sourced food; they also produce an ale and a bitter in their microbrewery. § *Nether Wasdale • Map C5 • 019467 26200*

Ritson's Bar
Packed to the rafters with hikers, Ritson's is a real hub in this remote valley. They offer a good range of beers and a lovely beer garden. Ritson's also serves large dinners that are simple but satisfying. § *Wasdale Head Inn • Map D5 • 019467 26229*

Zest Restaurant
A swish restaurant on the edge of Whitehaven, serving substantial modern British food. There is a funky sister café in town by the harbour. § *Low Road, Whitehaven • Map A4 • 01946 692848 • £££*

The Beacon Café
Sited at the base of the tower and offering nice harbour views, this is a handy daytime stop for substantial and tasty sandwiches and salads. § *The Beacon, Whitehaven • Map A4*

Gosforth Hall Inn
A tall and imposing 17th-century house, Gosforth Hall is full of quirky architectural detail. Acclaimed for its locally brewed ale and a pleasant beer garden. The restaurant offers hearty fare. § *Gosforth • Map B6 • 019467 25322*

Lakeland Habit Café
This cute daytime village café is a good spot for combining a coffee with a viewing of the Viking cross in the churchyard. The food is suited to different budgets and Sundays are dedicated to whole roasts. § *Gosforth • Map B6 • 019467 25232*

Low Wood Hall
A family-run hotel set in large gardens and woodland overlooking Nether Wasdale. Low Wood Hall is one of the few upmarket options in the area. § *Nether Wasdale • Map C5 • 019467 26100 • ££*

The Screes Inn
With good pub food, a log fire, real ales and a verdant village setting, this is one of the most popular inns in the area. § *Nether Wasdale • Map C5 • 019467 26262*

For a guide to restaurant prices **See p71.**

STREETSMART

THE LAKE DISTRICT'S TOP 10

Left **Trekkers in waterproof gear** Centre **Springtime daffodils** Right **A National Trust property**

Planning Your Trip

1 What to Pack
One thing you are almost sure to encounter in the Lake District is rain, so carry good waterproof clothing, boots and walking gear. A water bottle is handy at all times, as is sunscreen and a hat for hilltop walks. Even the warmest days can end with chilly evenings, so remember to bring a fleece or a jersey.

2 When to Go
Easter and bank holidays see large numbers of people making their way to the Lake District. The narrow roads become jammed and accommodation is hard to come by. Summer is the best time to visit the Cumbrian coast, although it is quite crowded with domestic travellers. Spring is a wonderful season to visit, with banks of daffodils in bloom, and autumn sees the trees and bracken on the fellsides turn a rich shade of russet.

3 Passports and Visas
Visitors from EU nations can visit the UK without a visa. It is advisable for all others to check with the British embassy in their home country to find out the requirements for a stay in the UK. To check whether you will need a visa, see www.ukvisas.gov.uk

4 Customs Regulations
Contact the UK Border Agency (www.ukba. homeoffice.gov.uk) for restrictions on what you can bring in and out of the UK. Visitors from outside the EU can make VAT-free purchases.

5 Insurance
It is always wise to take out insurance before you travel. Study the policy if you are planning to undertake high-risk sports. Make sure you are covered for baggage loss, theft and medical emergencies. Britain's National Health Service gives free emergency treatment, but you will have to pay for specialist care and prescription drugs. Keep your receipts for reimbursement.

6 Driving Licence
People from European Community and European Economic Area countries can use their driving licence in the UK. Travellers from other countries should check www.direct. gov.uk to find out their entitlements. UK citizens have to provide relevant documents and a photo ID when hiring a car.

7 Time Difference
From late October to late March, Greenwich Mean Time (GMT) prevails. The clocks go forward an hour in late March, marking the start of British Summer Time (BST), though the weather might tell a different story. GMT is five hours ahead of US Eastern Standard Time, and one or two hours behind most European countries.

8 Electrical Appliances
The supply throughout the United Kingdom is 240 volts AC. It you are coming from outside the UK you will need to buy a plug adaptor, which is readily available.

9 Children's Needs
The Lake District is well geared up for families, with many attractions for children *(see pp56–7)*. Nappy-changing facilities are available everywhere, and many restaurants and pubs have kids' menus. In some pubs, visitors with children will need to use a family room or the pub garden. Before booking, check with your hotel to see if children are welcome or if they have more economical family rooms.

10 Membership Cards
Students, children and senior citizens may get significant discounts at visitor attractions and on local and national transport (although you will need to buy a travel card). Members of National Trust and English Heritage can visit their properties for free, with the added benefit of free parking.

Left **Tourist bus** Centre **Sailboats on Lake Windermere** Right **Cycling around the Lake District**

🔟 Getting There and Around

1 By Air
Overseas visitors can fly to London and then take the train to Kendal or Windermere (via Oxenholme) from the capital's Euston Station. Travellers can also fly to Manchester. From Manchester Airport, there are direct local train services to Kendal and Windermere.

2 By Train
Taking the train is a quick and scenic way to reach the region. Virgin Trains operates the west coast mainline service between London (Euston Station) and Glasgow (Glasgow Central Station). Depending on your destination, you can change at Carlisle and Penrith (for the north) or Oxenholme and Lancaster (for the south).

3 By Coach
Visitors can access this region on a daily service to Windermere from London's Victoria Coach Station. Online ticket prices can be very low if you book in advance, but be prepared for an eight-hour journey.

4 By Car
You can reach the Lakes by car from the M6 motorway. However, road works and delays can make the M6 tedious during holiday season. An easier option is to take the train to Kendal and hire a car there.

5 By Local Bus
A number of good bus routes link the various small settlements in the Lake District. For example, you can take the train to Windermere and then very easily continue on to Ambleside, Grasmere and Keswick by bus. The Borrowdale Rambler bus in the northwestern Lakes follows the region's most scenic route. Ask at tourist offices or on the buses about daily or weekly discount tickets.

6 By Local Trains
Onward travel from Oxenholme to Kendal and Windermere is possible on the branch line, which has a regular and speedy service. The Furness and Cumbrian branch line between Lancaster and Carlisle, takes visitors around the Cumbrian coast; convenient stops include Barrow-in-Furness, Ravenglass, St Bees and Whitehaven.

7 By Local Ferries
Taking a ferry can be a really useful way of getting around the larger lakes. It is also a picturesque and fun way to travel and experience the lakes. The most substantial ferry services are available on Windermere, Coniston, Derwent Water and Ullswater, ranging from historic steamers to more utilitarian crafts.

8 By Bicycle
You will need to be tough to negotiate the high passes in the Lake District on a bicycle. But, as long as you are kitted out with a helmet, waterproofs and plenty of water, this can be a terrific way to get around. Visitors can hire a bike at all the main settlements in the Lakes.

9 On Foot
The Lake District is crisscrossed with long-distance walking routes such as the Coast-To-Coast Walk, the Cumbria Way and the Cumbrian Coastal Way, as well as other smaller trails. With an Ordnance Survey map you can have a wonderful time exploring the region on foot and staying in camp sites, farmhouses or B&Bs. Alternatively, find a specialist tour operator who will book your accommodation and transport your luggage for you as you walk.

10 By Organized Excursion
Many tour operators will customize your holiday, whether you want to travel by minibus around prehistoric sights, ride a horse across the fells or concentrate on fishing, riding, watersports or hiking. Usually all you have to do is get to the Lakes, and the tour company will arrange all the practical details.

Left **Stormy weather** Centre **Wainwright Guides** Right **Maps on sale outside Sam Read's Bookshop**

TOP 10 Sources of Information

1 Tourist Information Centres

Cumbria Tourism has offices scattered throughout the region, where you can get hold of maps, book accommodation, and get advice on local sites and interesting walks. There is more advice on getting the best from your stay at the Lake District National Park website: www.lake-district.gov.uk. *www.cumbriatourism.org*

2 Local Bookshops

The Lake District is a haven for interesting independent bookshops, which are stacked with local fiction, guides for walks, maps and histories of the region. They are a good alternative source of inspiration and ideas for your travels; Sam Read's Bookshop in Grasmere is one of the best in the area *(see p9).*

3 National Park Visitor Centre

The visitor centre at Brockhole makes for an educational and fun visit. There are exhibits on the region's flora and fauna, as well as an adventure park, an Arts and Crafts garden, a café serving Cumbrian home-baked treats and a shop selling locally-made products. *Brockhole, Windermere • Map N1 • 015394 46601 • www.lakedistrict.gov.uk*

4 Local Newspapers

Cumbria has a lively local news network with Kendal's *Westmorland Gazette*, founded in 1818, being the newspaper you are most likely to encounter. Visit their website www.thewestmorelandgazette.co.uk to bring yourself up to date with the daily headlines. The *Cumberland & Westmorland Herald* (www.cwherald.com) is another local title.

5 Local Radio

The local BBC channel is BBC Radio Cumbria, available at 95.6FM, 96.1FM and 104.1FM frequencies, offering listeners updates on the news, weather and sports, as well as interviews on the arts, nature and local events.

6 Cumbria Life

Cumbria Life is a bi-monthly glossy magazine, with lots of useful information about places to eat and drink in the region. *www.cumbrialife.co.uk*

7 Websites

Apart from the tourist board site, the single most useful resource for the Lake District is the encyclopedic website www.visitcumbria.com – a directory of sites on everything from farm shops to hot air ballooning to cinemas.

8 Maps

The best maps available are those from the Ordnance Survey (OS) range; either the pink Landranger (1: 50,000) or the more detailed orange Explorer series (1: 25,000). Other options include Collins' "walking maps" which provide advice to hikers and mark paths and youth hostels.

9 Weather

Most places to stay in the Lake District, from upmarket hotels to hostels, normally post the next day's weather at the reception. It is definitely worth scanning this if you are planning a hike or any other outdoor activity. You can also call the National Park Authority Weatherline on 0844 846 2444. Additionally, the Metereological Office website is generally reliable. *www.metoffice.gov.uk*

10 Wainwright Guides

Alfred Wainwright compiled his seven classic Pictorial Guides to the Lakeland Fells between 1952 and 1966. Illustrated by the author, they have been sensitively updated. They still provide practical and personal guidance for a walk in the region.

Left **Postbox** Centre **Sign for Internet** Right **WiFi café**

🔟 Banking and Communications

1 Money
The UK currency, emblazoned with the Queen's head, is the pound sterling, divided into 100 pence (p). Notes are available in denominations of £5, £10, £20 and £50. Coins are divided into 1p, 2p, 5p, 10p, 20p, 50p, £1 and £2.

2 Banks
British banks are mostly open between 9:30am and 5:30pm from Monday to Friday. You can also withdraw money from ATMs outside banks. Most of the major towns have ATMs of at least one major international bank, including HSBC, Abbey, Barclays and Natwest. ATMs can also be found inside some grocery stores and petrol stations.

3 Currency Exchange
There are Bureaux de Change in Barrow-in-Furness, Kendal, Whitehaven and Workington. Otherwise, you can also try the larger post offices for exchanging traveller's cheques and currency.

4 Credit Cards
Credit cards are accepted in shops, hotels and bigger restaurants, but you may not be able to use them in B&Bs, pubs and camp sites. Avoid using credit cards for cash withdrawals, as interest rates are high.

5 Postal Services
Many post offices in rural areas of Britain have closed in recent times, but you can still find some small branches in village shops, and the main towns will all have a post office. They open office on weekdays, and on Saturday mornings. Stamps are available, either singly or in books of 6 or 12, with newsagents and large supermarkets.
⊛ www.postoffice.co.uk

6 Postal Charges
Postal charges depend on the size of your letter, and whether you send it first or second class – this determines the speed at which it will reach its destination. You can pay extra for guaranteed next-day delivery, or to insure valuable contents. See the Post Office website for more.
⊛ www.postoffice.co.uk

7 Internet Access
Most of the upmarket hotels, restaurants, B&Bs, and cafés in the Lakes have Internet as well as WiFi facilities, sometimes for a fee. You can access the Internet at all YHA hostels, although the rates are very high. Public libraries usually offer free Internet, but for limited time periods. Some tourist centres also have a few terminals for public use.

8 Mobile Phones
Bear in mind, especially if you're out walking in a remote area, that mobile coverage is limited in the Lakes District. Signals are often lost, so do not rely on a mobile phone to get you out of trouble when you are walking. The larger service providers usually have better connectivity. If the weather changes dramatically, turn around and leave the summit for another day and in case of emergencies try to locate a public phone.

9 Telephones
You will find phone boxes (including some of the traditional red ones) scattered throughout the Lakes. They take coins, phonecards and sometimes even credit cards. Phonecards are available at most village shops and pubs. Phone booths are useful while travelling in remote areas.

10 Dialling Codes
Use the 5- or 6-digit area code when you are calling fixed landline numbers within the Lake District unless you are calling a number with the same code. If you are calling from outside the UK, dial the access code, and then the area code without the initial zero. To call abroad, dial 00 and then the country code. Directory enquiries are on 118 500 (domestic) and 118 505 (overseas).

Left **Rowing a boat in the Lakes** Centre **Pharmacy** Right **Woman traveller with a map**

⓾ Security and Health

1 Emergencies
Call 999 for emergency assistance from the police, fire or ambulance departments. Calls to 999 are free.

2 Theft
Theft and crime in general is not a big issue in the Lakes. Take normal precautions about locking your car and not leaving bags unattended and you should be fine. Report any thefts to the police as you will need a crime report number to make an insurance claim.

3 Lost Property
Try the nearest police station if you lose your personal property. Contact the relevant transport company if you leave something behind on public transport. In order to prevent any loss of luggage during treks and outdoor activities, leave your bags with the hotel or hostel, which usually has a room for storage.

4 Hospitals
Call 999 for any medical emergency. The following hospitals have emergency departments: Royal Lancaster Infirmary (Ashton Road, Lancaster), Furness General Hospital (Dalton Lane, Barrow-in-Furness), Cumberland Infirmary (Newtown Road, Carlisle, Cumbria), the West Cumberland Hospital (Whitehaven) and Westmorland General Hospital, Kendal.

5 Pharmacies
All the main towns and settlements in the region have a pharmacy (usually open 9am–5pm, Mon–Sat); if they are closed they will have contact details of the nearest alternative outlet posted. Boots, the biggest high-street pharmacy in the UK, has branches all over the Lake District. All UK pharmacists are well trained and able to give advice on basic medical matters if you are unable to see a doctor.

6 Dentists
You have to be registered to see an NHS (National Health Service) dentist. However, in an emergency, call the dental helpline on 0845-063-1188.

7 Insect Bites
Small black ticks can attach themselves to your skin and cannot be brushed off; they may also carry Lyme disease. If you see a tick on your body, contact a doctor or pharmacist promptly. Bites from the harmless but intensely annoying midges (small flies which congregate around still water in summer) are common in the Lakes. Cover your arms and legs with long sleeved shirts and trousers, or use a good insect repellent. ℡ *0845 4647*
• *www.nhsdirect.nhs.uk*

8 Safety in the Water
All outlets where boats and canoes can be rented should prioritize your safety, giving you a life jacket and a briefing on what to do if you get into trouble. While this region does have some lovely swimming spots, these are recommended for competent adult swimmers only. Do bear in mind that the Lakes are quite deep and can shelve suddenly.

9 Climbing Hazards
Climbing is a popular and challenging sport in the Lake District, but it is also potentially dangerous. The isolated nature of many mountains in the Lakes means that help may not be readily at hand in case of an emergency. It is safer to climb as part of a team, or on an excursion with a qualified instructor. Climbing practice and guidance is available at the Lakeland Climbing Centre in Kendal.

10 Women Travellers
The Lake District is a very safe place for women travelling alone or in a group. Generally speaking, the people you meet, locals and visitors alike, are friendly and open. If women do suffer trouble or aggression in any form, they can report it to the local authorities and call 999 in case of any emergencies.

Left **Narrow mountain road** Centre **Square crowded with cars** Right **Pub signage**

TOP 10 Things to Avoid

1 School and Bank Holidays
The Lake District is hugely popular with families, and on public and school holidays the roads can be very crowded with all the hotels, bed & breakfasts and hostels full to bursting and cafés and restaurants completely booked up. Easter is a particularly busy time. If you plan to wander "lonely as a cloud" in the Lakes, make sure you avoid the holiday period.

2 Driving
It is perfectly easy and more fun to take a combination of trains, buses, cars, cycles or even walk to make your way around the Lakes. It can be stressful to drive here, especially at busy times, as the roads are narrow and the towns and villages of this area were not built with automated vehicles in mind.

3 Driving on Minor Roads at Night
Many of the roads in the Lake District are narrow, unlit and precipitous, making night driving stressful at best and dangerous at worst. In particular, high passes such as the Hardknott Pass should be avoided after nightfall as the gradients are very steep with loose gravel and an uneven surface that can cause accidents.

4 Late Bookings
The Lakes are hugely popular with British and overseas visitors, so visitors should book their accommodation quite far in advance to avoid disappointment and hassles. It is not advisable to turn up at a hostel without prior reservations as most of them are booked by large groups, even on weekdays.

5 Hiking Unprepared
Do not set out on a hike unless you are properly dressed, well shod and stocked with food, water, sunscreen and a basic first aid kit. You will also need an Ordnance Survey map, a good hiking guide and a compass. Do not rely on finding signposts or being able to consult other walkers – the mountains here are on a large scale and the pathways are not always clearly defined.

6 Stormy Weather
Before undertaking any kind of outdoor activity, do check the local weather reports. And even if you are setting out on a clear, sunny day, always carry a waterproof jacket as the weather can change fast in these parts.

7 Hiring a Car on Weekends
Car hire outlets in the Lake District are few, and they are mostly closed on weekends (except Saturday mornings), making it impossible to pick up or leave cars during this time.

8 The Crowds
Settlements such as Grasmere (see pp8–9) are extremely popular, attracting large crowds through the year. If you want to get away from it all, travel further west in the region, or consider the isolated coastline and intriguing towns such as Cockermouth, outside the national park area.

9 Bad Food
Eating habits in the Lake District have transformed in recent years, with a strong emphasis on fresh and local food. Pub food, in particular, has benefited from creative chefs and good ingredients. But it is still possible to find good old British stodge, particularly in the more staid hotels. Visitors are advised to scour hotel menus carefully before ordering anything.

10 Getting Stranded on a Mountain
Always tell someone at your hotel or hostel accommodation where you are going before setting out on a major excursion, climb or cycling trip. Do not rely on your mobile phone alone to get you out of a fix, as coverage is limited in this area.

Left **Travellers in waterproof jackets** Centre **Sign welcoming walkers** Right **Lake District maps**

🔟 Walking and Hiking Tips

1 Boots
The main advice is to wear in your boots before you go, to avoid blisters. In case of emergencies, carry plenty of plasters. High-fashion boots are not the best option and hikers should go to a reputable outdoor shop and buy thick socks to wear with their boots. Good boots give strong ankle support and are the best bet for long walks or treks.

2 Waterproofs
A breathable waterproof jacket with a hood should see you through the unpredictable weather in the Lakes. It is a good idea to invest in a pair of waterproof trousers or gaiters that are easy enough to keep bundled in your backpack, should bad weather strike. There are plenty of outdoor shops in the region, particularly in Ambleside, if you need to stock up on your waterproof gear.

3 Compass
A compass is a useful tool to help orient yourself in the Lakes. You can buy one in any of the local outdoor shops, and they will guide you on the simple process of using one in conjunction with your map.

4 Other Gear
Walking experts suggest layering your outdoor clothes as the best form of protection against the elements. Wear a synthetic base layer, then a fleece, and top it off with a waterproof jacket. Be sure to take enough food and water, a flask with a warm drink if possible, plus a torch and a whistle for emergencies.

5 Guidebooks
Local tourist offices and bookshops will equip you with leaflets and local guidebooks for walks in the region. However, it is always advisable to use these in conjunction with a relevant Ordnance Survey Explorer map, and a compass. The widely available Wainwright guides (see p41) describe the classic fell routes.

6 Maps
The best choice for serious walkers is the orange Ordnance Survey (OS) Explorer series (1:25,000) scale. The Collins' "walking maps" (1:63,360) scale also mark paths, tracks and youth hostels.

7 Weather
The weather in the Lakes changes rapidly so check the daily weather forecast in the newspaper. For the most up-to-date information, call Weatherline on 0844-846-2444. Also check the timings for tides if you are planning a walk along the shore. If conditions are poor, go to a pub instead of attempting a precipitous walk or climb.

8 Inform Someone of Where you are Going
This is the most basic but also extremely important advice. If you are planning any kind of major outdoor outing then tell someone where you are going. The best option would be the proprietor of the accommodation where you are staying.

9 Emergencies
If someone in your party is injured when you are walking, call the police on 999 – they will contact the nearest Mountain Rescue Team. Use your map to give as precise a location as possible. Otherwise, try to dress wounds to stem bleeding, ensure the injured person's breathing is unobstructed, and keep them and yourself warm and sheltered.

10 Mobile-Phone Coverage
Mobile coverage is limited in the Lakes, and particularly unreliable in the mountains. However, make sure your phone is fully charged before you go out for an excursion. In case of an accident, call the emergency services and keep your phone switched on so that they can contact you again if necessary.

Left **Buttermere camp site** Centre **Fairtrade sign** Right **YHA hostel**

🔟 Accommodation and Dining Tips

1 Renting Properties

Renting a property with friends can be a fun experience and more economical than renting rooms in a hotel. Try: www.holidaylettings.co.uk/cumbria-lake-district; www.muncaster.co.uk; www.ruralretreats.co.uk; www.iknow-lakedistrict.co.uk; www.holiday-rentals.co.uk; or www.landmarktrust.org.uk for information on property rentals. Another good option is block-booking one of the region's very good youth hostels. See www.yha.org.uk for more details.

2 Advance Booking

It is advisable to book hotels at least a month in advance during holiday periods, especially Easter.

3 Farmstays

This is a good option for children and provides bed and breakfast facilities, but on a working farm. Lambing time is great fun and most farmers will welcome help, although there is no obligation. For ideas try www.lakedistricts.co.uk/accommodation/Lakes/farmstays

4 Camping

The Lake District's camp sites are excellent and have wonderfully scenic locations. They range from luxurious sites with attached toilets, underfloor heating, onsite restaurants and snug yurts (a large, circular tent-like structure covered with felt) for hire to simple tap and field sites. The major sites, particularly the three National Trust ones, fill up quickly on sunny weekends and during holidays. You cannot book ahead at most camp sites; just show up early and try your luck.

5 Youth Hostels

Youth hostels are an affordable option in the Lakes as well as a good way to meet other travellers. The cheapest option is a shared dorm, but you can also hire twin or family rooms in most hostels. YHA (Youth Hostels Association) is the main organization – you need to be a member to stay in a YHA hostel, but can join on the spot for a fee of £15.95. The Lakes area also has many independent hostels that can be cheaper and better equipped than the YHA alternative. 🔌 www.yha.org.uk • www.independenthostelguide.com

6 Bunkhouses and Camping Barns

If you do not want to lug a tent around and are happy to rough it, then the rugged bunkhouses and camping barns scattered around this area are a good option. See www.findabunkhouse.co.uk and www.lakelandcampingbarns.

co.uk. You need to be prepared for minimal facilities and carry your own bedding.

7 Upmarket Restaurants

The Lakes have some excellent restaurants and a sprinkling of Michelin stars. The finest eateries can be found in the region's luxury hotels. An opulent lunch will often cost less than dinner. Some of the hotels have a dress code and so it's advisable to dress smartly for a meal out.

8 Local Produce

The best restaurants and cafés in the region make the most of the excellent local produce, which ranges from Herdwick lamb to farmhouse icecream.

9 Fairtrade Cafés

The Lake District as a whole takes Fairtrade (where the produce is directly purchased from the growers) seriously, and several cafés in the region are Fairtrade only. Look out for the swirling green and blue symbol on a black background.

10 Fish'n'chips

When you have been out walking all day, there is nothing that fills the stomach like good old fish'n'chips slathered with salt and vinegar and served with a pile of mushy peas on the side.

Left **Gilpin Lodge** Centre **Interior, Rothay Garden** Right **Miller Howe Hotel**

Luxury Hotels

1 Holbeck Ghyll Country House Hotel

A superb country house retreat with Arts and Crafts details, this hotel has luxurious bedrooms, sweeping views of the Langdale pikes and incomparable food. All this plus a really warm welcome from the proud owners. ◎ *Holbeck Lane, Windermere • Map N2 • 015394 32375 • www.holbeckghyll.com • ££££*

2 The Samling

An 18th-century whitewashed building, Samling is perched high above Windermere in a 67-acre (27-ha) estate. It prefers to avoid the country house designation and calls itself a luxury hotel in the country instead. The accent is on comfort and understated elegance. ◎ *Ambleside Road, Windermere • Map N2 • 015394 31922 • www.thesamling hotel.co.uk • £££££*

3 Rothay Garden

This contemporary boutique-hotel is housed in a handsome stone building on the edge of Grasmere. There is a lovely lawn dotted with quirky benches. Dove Cottage is nearby, the staff are friendly and the food is excellent. Ask for the loft suites with great views. ◎ *Broadgate, Grasmere • Map E5 • 015394 35334 • www.rothaygarden.com • ££££*

4 Gilpin Lodge

This lodge is very much a family affair – it is run and staffed by people who clearly love their jobs. This attitude is reflected in the decor, food and comfort of the place. The garden suites are modern and elegant, backed by moors and woodland. Their restaurant is close at hand. ◎ *Crook Road, Windermere • Map N2 • 00800 2000 0002 • www.relaischateaux. com/gilpin • ££££*

5 Armathwaite Hall

A fine country house hotel and award-winning spa on the edge of Bassenthwaite Lake. Armathwaite Hall is set in 400 acres (162 ha) and facilities include a gym, pool, sauna and steam rooms. ◎ *Bassenthwaite Lake • Map D2 • 017687 76551 • www.armathwaite-hall.com • £££££*

6 Linthwaite House Hotel

Among the top Lakes' hotels, Linthwaite House boasts wonderful views of Windermere. The decor is elegant and the emphasis is on unstuffy comfort and attentive service. ◎ *Crook Road, Windermere • Map N2 • 015394 88600 • www.linthwaite.com • ££££*

7 Langdale Chase

An opulent country hotel, Langdale Chase features a wonderfully atmospheric oak-panelled interior, tennis courts, croquet and an excellent restaurant. ◎ *Windermere • Map N2 • 015394 32201 • www.langdalechase.co.uk • ££££*

8 Sharrow Bay

Established in 1948, Sharrow Bay is a comfortable old-style retreat. The Michelin-starred restaurant enhances its reputation. Pudding aficionados will be interested in the claim that sticky toffee pudding was invented here. ◎ *Ullswater • Map G4 • 00800 2000 0002 • www.relaischateaux.com/ sharrow • £££££*

9 Miller Howe Hotel

This Arts and Crafts house has been lovingly restored, with fabulous furniture and plush rooms, some with breathtaking views of Windermere. The food here is superb, making the room-plus-dinner tariff worth considering. ◎ *Rayrigg Road, Windermere • Map N2 • 015394 42536 • www.millerhowe.com • ££££*

10 Overwater Hall

A family-owned place and a Lakes' favourite, Overwater Hall is set in a listed 18th-century mansion. Backed by Skiddaw, this lovely hotel has a traditional yet modern decor and is surrounded by 18 acres (7 ha) of gardens and woodland. ◎ *Ireby • Map D1 • 017687 76566 • www.overwaterhall.co.uk • ££££*

Price Categories		
For a standard double room per night, inclusive of taxes and any additional charges.	£ under £80
	££ £80–£120
	£££ £120–£170
	££££ £170–£220
	£££££ over £220

Left **The Brown Horse Inn** Centre **Lindeth Fell**

Mid-Range Hotels and Inns

1 Waterhead Hotel
Located on the shores of Windermere, the Waterhead has been converted into a boutique "townhouse" style hotel, with contemporary fittings and features. ◉ Ambleside • Map F5 • 08458 504 503 • www. elh.co.uk • £££

2 Eltermere Country House
A country house by the lake near the enchanting village of Elterwater, Eltermere Country House is decked out with modern furnishings. There is a spa, sauna, steam room, on site jacuzzi and tennis courts. ◉ Elterwater • Map E5 • 015394 37207 • www. eltermere.co.uk • £££

3 Drunken Duck
This lovely old inn north of Hawkshead has been stylishly modernized, but has retained old features such as the exposed beams and wooden fireplaces. The restaurant, serving modern British food (see p38), attracts visitors from all over. ◉ Barngates, Ambleside • Map F5 • 015394 36347 • www.drunkenduckinn.co. uk • £££

4 The Brown Horse Inn
A comfortable road-side inn in the Winster valley, the Brown Horse has nine en-suite rooms, flat-screen TVs, oak beams and cosy furnishings. It is distinguished by a terrific restaurant that uses produce from their own farm. ◉ Sunny Bank Road, Winster, Windermere • Map N2 • 015394 43443 • www.thebrownhorseinn. co.uk • ££

5 The Punchbowl Inn
A venerable inn in the Lyth Valley that has been given a classic but thoroughly modern makeover, with stylish fabrics, Roberts radios, flat-screen TVs and roll-topped baths. It is also a great option for eating. ◉ Crosthwaite, Lyth Valley, near Kendal • Map N3 • 015395 68327 • www. the-punchbowl.co.uk • £££

6 Pheasant Inn
This rambling, low-beamed, fire-lit, white-washed inn is more than 500 years old. Originally a farmhouse, the Pheasant Inn has been fuctioning as an inn since 1778 and is a really atmospheric place to stay. ◉ Bassenthwaite Lake, Cockermouth • Map D2 • 017687 76234 • www. the-pheasant.co.uk • ££££

7 Lindeth Fell
Built in 1909, this handsome place over-looks Windermere. The family-run hotel gives a warm welcome to all its visitors; it is extremely comfortable and slightly old-fashioned in the best sense. A good choice if you plan to visit Blackwell (see p10), which is just a short walk away. ◉ Windermere • Map N2 • 015394 43286 • www. lindethfell.co.uk • £££

8 Swinside Lodge Hotel
A lovely Georgian hotel that combines country house elegance with a modern touch. The rooms look out to Cat Bells, Skiddaw and Blencathra, and the walks are superb. ◉ Newlands, Keswick • Map D3 • 017687 72948 • www.swinsidelodge-hotel.co.uk • ££££

9 Lancrigg
An interesting hotel option which specializes in organic, vegetarian food, and in providing a stress-free environment. Massage, reiki, medi-tation walks and other therapies are available. The rooms are bright and soothing, some with original plasterwork. ◉ Easedale, Grasmere • Map E5 • 015394 35317 • www.lancrigg.co.uk • ££££

10 Hazelbank
A grand mid-Victorian house surrounded by woodland in the lovely Borrowdale Valley, Hazelbank's original features include the old servants' bell. The rooms are very plush and warm. ◉ Borrowdale • Map D4 • 017687 77248 • www. hazelbankhotel.co.uk • £££

Left **Fair Rigg** Centre **Brathay Hall** Right **Waterwheel Guesthouse**

TOP 10 B&Bs

1 Fair Rigg
A friendly and efficient B&B, Fair Rigg occupies a Victorian stone house high above Bowness and looks out to Lake Windermere and the surrounding fells. The rooms feature traditional décor and are impeccably clean and cosy. ⊗ *Ferry View, Bowness-on-Windermere • Map N2 • 015394 43941 • www.fairrigg.co.uk • £*

2 Brathay Hall
This Georgian mansion is set in 360 acres (146 ha) of mature woodland and rolling pastures, and lies at the head of Lake Windermere. The accommodation is suitable for individuals, couples, families or groups and ranges from dormitory-style rooms to luxury en-suite. ⊗ *Troutbeck • Map N1 • 015394 33041 • www.brathay.org.uk • £–£££*

3 Waterwheel Guesthouse
A little guesthouse in one of the most picturesque buildings in a pretty town, the Waterwheel Guesthouse is a 300-year-old cottage looking out to rushing Stock Ghyll and a wooden waterwheel opposite. The three bedrooms are en suite, two have Victorian clawfoot baths. ⊗ *3 Bridge Street, Ambleside • Map F5 • 015394 33286 • www.waterwheel-ambleside.co.uk • ££*

4 Esthwaite Old Hall
A gorgeous, atmospheric 400-year-old stone building, Esthwaite Old Hall looks out onto Esthwaite Water and is just over a mile from Hawkshead. This guest house offers tranquility and comfort. ⊗ *Hawkshead • Map M2 • 015394 36007 • www.esthwaiteoldhall.co.uk • £*

5 Crosthwaite House
A grand, cream-coloured Georgian house, Crosthwaithe House is located in the lush Lyth Valley. The owners provide a terrific breakfast, as well as advice on the local area. It is good for walks and discovering the excellent nearby pubs. ⊗ *Crosthwaite, near Kendal • Map N3 • 01539 568 264 • www.crosthwaitehouse.co.uk • ££*

6 Yew Tree Farm
Owned by Beatrix Potter in the 1930s, this picturesque 17th-century farmhouse was used as a location for the film *Miss Potter* (2006). There is an oak staircase, ancient beams and goose-down duvets to keep you warm at night. ⊗ *Coniston • Map M2 • 015394 41433 • www.yewtree-farm.com • ££*

7 Cote Howe
A licensed organic guesthouse, Cote Howe is a long, low white-washed building dating back to the 16th century. They serve a fantastic full English breakfast and run a tea room on site that is open daily. ⊗ *Rydal • Map F5 • 015394 32765 • www.cotehow.co.uk • ££*

8 Yewfield
This vegetarian B&B in Hawkshead has 13 chic rooms. Surrounded by 80 acres (32 ha) of land, this Victorian-Gothic house includes wild-flower meadows and a coppice garden. Yewfield also stages classical music concerts. ⊗ *Hawkshead Hill, Hawkshead • Map M2 • 015394 36765 • www.yewfield.co.uk • ££*

9 Seatoller House
A 17th-century house with lovely rustic-style rooms, Seatoller House preserves the rural peace by having no TV or radio. It is well placed for walks up Great Gable and Scafell, or just a potter round Borrowdale. ⊗ *Seatoller, Borrowdale • Map D4 • 017687 77218 • www.seatollerhouse.co.uk • £££*

10 Acorn House
A grand Georgian structure, Acorn House has traditionally furnished rooms – three have four-poster beds. It is perfect for visiting nearby attractions. ⊗ *Ambleside Road, Keswick • Map U6 • 017687 72553 • www.acornhousehotel.co.uk • ££*

Left **A camping barn** Right **Wasdale Head Inn**

Price Categories

For a standard double room per night (taxes and breakfast) and for a room at an inn, per night (breakfast not included).

£	under £80
££	£80–£120
£££	£120–£170
££££	£170–£220
£££££	over £220

₀₁₀ Hikers' Hotels & Camping Barns

1 Langstrath Country Inn

Ancient Stonethwaite in Borrowdale is the backdrop for the family-run Langstrath Country Inn. Converted from a miner's cottage built in 1590, the inn has eight cosy en-suite rooms, an open fire in the lounge and dishes up good local food. ◎ *Stonethwaite, Borrowdale • Map D4 • 017687 77239 • www. thelangstrath.com • ££*

2 Old Dungeon Ghyll

Set in the spectacular Langdale Valley at the foot of the fells, Old Dungeon Ghyll has been providing a warm haven for walkers for 300 years. It is old-fashioned but comfortable, and is home to the excellent Hiker's Bar, which serves real ales and filling food. ◎ *Great Langdale • Map E5 • 015394 37272 • www. odg.co.uk • ££*

3 Wasdale Head Inn

Situated at the end of the narrow road through Wasdale, this inn boasts the best views in Britain. It has been a sanctuary for walkers since hiking and climbing became popular here. There are ten bedrooms, plus two roomy apartments and seven self-catering apartments in the neighbouring barn. Good dinners are served in the dining room. Try Ritson's Bar for the hearty pub

grub and real ale. ◎ *Wasdale Head, near Gosforth • Map D5 • 019467 26229 • www. wasdale.com • ££*

4 Seathwaite Camping Barn

Located on a working farm with a camp site and a barn, Seathwaite is renowned for its wild beauty. There are 18 bunk beds and a simple kitchen. You are better off self-catering as this is a remote spot. It is perfect for walks up Scafell Pike and Great Gable. ◎ *Seathwaite, Borrowdale • Map D4 • 017687 77394 • £7 per person*

5 Wythmoor

A 19th-century barn that is less basic than some other camping barns, Wythmoor has toilets and showers with solar-heated water and electricity provided by a wind turbine. There is also a barbecue area. ◎ *Wythmoor Farm, Lambrigg, Kendal • Map Q2 • 01768 774301 • £8.50 per person*

6 Swallow Barn

Set in a 17th-century farm, this barn is in the Loweswater Valley. There is electricity, toilets, showers and a water heater. Bring your own food and sleeping bags. ◎ *Waterend Farm, Loweswater, Cockermouth • Map C3 • 01946 861465 • £8.50 per person*

7 Fell End

A camping barn for adventurous travellers, Fell End has wood-stoves and no electricity. It is a good idea to bring a torch or a lamp, although tea lights are provided. ◎ *Coniston • Map M2 • 01229 716340 • £8.50 per person*

8 Brotherswater Inn

A venerable old Lakes inn near the Kirkstone Pass, Brotherswater is traditional family-run place. Ideal for walks in the valley. ◎ *Brotherswater, Patterdale • Map F4 • 01768 482239 • www.sykeside. co.uk • £*

9 The Britannia Inn

Sitting pretty on the green in Elterwater, this 500-year-old inn is a good option for walkers who want a little comfort. The rooms have been refurbished, in old-English style. ◎ *Elterwater • Map E5 • 015394 37210 • www. britinn.net • ££*

10 The Traveller's Rest

This rugged old 16th-century coaching inn is perfect for exploring Grasmere and Dove Cottage, as well as for walking on the fells. The nine rooms are done up in a traditional style full of charm and character. The inn's pub serves a wide range of local ales. ◎ *N of Grasmere • Map E5 • 0500 600725 • www. lakedistrictinns.co.uk • ££*

Bring your own mat and sleeping bag for stays in camping barns. For more details see www.lakelandcampingbarns.co.uk

Left **Grasmere Independent Hostel** Centre **Patterdale hostel** Right **Elterwater youth hostel**

Youth Hostels

Ambleside YHA
While it might not be the most beautiful hostel in the Lakes, Ambleside enjoys a great location at the edge of Windermere. The facilities are decent, the views are dramatic and it offers a variety of watersports. It is also near most of Ambleside's attractions. ✎ *Waterhead, Ambleside • Map F6 • 0845 371 9620 • ££–££££*

Hawkshead YHA
Looking out over Esthwaite, this listed Regency mansion is a short distance from lovely Hawkshead. It is a good option for getting away from it all and there are some fine pubs just walking distance away. ✎ *Hawkshead • Map M2 • 0845 371 9321 • ££–£££*

New Ing Lodge
An independent hostel housed in a farm, New Ing Lodge has excellent facilities and two mixed dorms. The hostel offers meals on request and there is also a small kitchen. It is conveniently situated on the route of the Coast-to-Coast walk as well as the Westmoreland Way. ✎ *Main Street, Shap • Map H4 • 01931 716719 • £££ • www.newinglodge.co.uk*

Elterwater YHA
Housed in a gorgeous old farm building, this hostel is a friendly stop for outdoorsy types exploring the Langdale Valley. There is a river rushing by and the village is one of the most characterful in the Lakes. The renowned Britannia Inn is just a stroll away on the green. ✎ *Elterwater • Map E5 • 0845 371 9017 • £££*

Honister Hause
A rugged and isolated option for hikers exploring Borrowdale and Buttermere – this hostel sits on the high pass that links the two valleys. They provide breakfast, a packed lunch and dinner to hungry hikers. ✎ *Seatoller • Map D4 • 017687 77267 • £££*

Grasmere Independent Hostel
Regarded as the best hostel in the Lakes, this clean and snug place occupies a converted barn along a hillside above Grasmere. There is a great kitchen, a TV lounge with a circular viewing window overlooking the fells, and good facilities for washing and drying clothes. ✎ *Broadrayne Farm, Grasmere • Map E5 • 015394 35055 • www.grasmerehostel.co.uk • £££*

Cockermouth YHA
Set in a wonderful 17th-century watermill on the River Cocker, the hostel is a quiet and restful place. It is the ideal spot from which to explore the area. ✎ *Double Mills, Cockermouth • Map C2 • 0845 371 9313 • £££*

Patterdale YHA
This Ullswater hostel is lively and full of character. It boasts attractive rooms, comfortable beds, open fires and good breakfasts. It is ideal for hikes up to Helvellyn and for trips to the lakeside and the neighbourhood pubs. ✎ *Patterdale • Map F4 • 0845 371 9337 • £££*

Borrowdale YHA
This peaceful hostel is perfectly situated for access to some of the best hill walking in the Lake District. It is located on the River Derwent and on the footpath to Seatoller and is a handy stop if you are on the Coast-to-Coast walk or the Cumbria Way. It's a perfect base for exploring the lush attractions and handsome little settlements of Borrowdale. ✎ *Longthwaite, Borrowdale • Map D4 • 0845 371 9624 • £££*

Keswick YHA
An excellent modern hostel, Keswick YHA is housed in a historic whitewashed riverside woollen mill near the town centre. It is a big and friendly place with a pool table, good washing facilities and Internet access. ✎ *Station Road, Keswick • Map T5 • 0845 371 9746 • ££££*

Left **Yurt, Full Circle** Centre **Syke Farm camp site**

🔟 Camp Sites

Full Circle
Book ahead for space at Full Circle – the felt yurts with their beautiful bright painted doors are very popular. They sit in the grounds of Rydal Hall, with easy access to Grasmere and Ambleside via the scenic Coffin Route. Each yurt has a wood stove, making it a snug and practical choice for a winter visit. ◈ *Rydal Hall, Ambleside • Map F5 • 07975 671928 • www.lake-district-yurts. co.uk • £££££ per yurt for a long weekend*

Gillside
A fabulous location on the fellside above Glenridding makes Gillside a great choice for walkers. It is a friendly farmhouse site with basic facilities, but you can buy your milk and eggs at the farm and stroll down to the village for shops, pubs and trips on Ullswater. ◈ *Gillside Farm, Glenridding • Map F4 • 01768 482346 • £*

Side Farm
Sitting pretty on the southern shore of Ullswater, Side Farm is a lovely farm site. The entrance to the camp site has an impressive traditional bank barn, and a teashop dishing out tea, coffee and home-made cakes. It is a great base for walkers and cyclists. ◈ *Patterdale, Ullswater • Map F4 • 01768 482337 • £*

Low Wray
Run by the National Trust, Low Wray is on the shores of Windermere. There is a small premium to pitch your tents by the water. You can hire canoes, kayaks and mountain bikes nearby, and the camp site reception has leaflets on hiking and cycling routes. ◈ *Low Wray, near Ambleside • Map F6 • 015394 63862 • www. nationaltrust.org.uk • ££*

Wasdale
Another National Trust-run site, this one is for serious walkers and climbers. This area is dotted with trees, and steep fell walls rise above, providing some of the best hiking in the country. ◈ *Wasdale Head • Map D5 • 019467 26220 • www.nationaltrust.org.uk • ££*

Syke Farm
An attractive camp site, accessed via a little wooden footbridge. There are walks right on the doorstep (including Haystacks, Wainwright's favourite fell). There are a couple of great pubs nearby and the home-made farm ice cream is excellent. ◈ *Buttermere Village • Map C4 • 017687 70222 • £*

Hollows Farm
Tucked away in a lush valley, Hollows Farm is a truly idyllic spot. The gently sloping meadow is fringed by a stream and surrounded by a forest and fells. It is a basic site, but perfect for nature lovers. ◈ *Grange-in-Borrowdale • Map D4 • 017687 77298 • www. hollowsfarm.co.uk • £*

Sykeside
Magnificent mountain views are the defining characteristic of Sykeside camp site, with enticing fells such as High Hartsop Dodd providing a great backdrop. There is also a bunkhouse called the Barn End Bar. ◈ *Brotherswater, Patterdale • Map F4 • 01768 482239 • ££*

The Quiet Site
This pretty carbon-neutral site has plenty of wet-weather diversions, including a fabulous Gothic bar converted from an ancient barn. There is also a pool table, table football, soft play area and a playground. ◈ *Ullswater • Map F3 • 07768 727016 • www. thequietsite.co.uk • ££*

Fisherground
Fisherground is heaven for kids with an adventure playground – it is also a request stop for the lovely little trains of the Ravenglass & Eskdale steam railway. Each pitch has a bowl for lighting fires, making it magical for adults too. ◈ *Fellside Cottage, Eskdale • Map C6 • 019467 23349 • www.fisherground campsite.co.uk • £*

General Index

Page numbers in **bold** type refer to main entries

Index

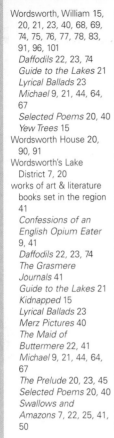

Acknowledgments

Author and photographer
Helena Smith is a travel writer and photographer (helenasmith. co.uk). She wrote the *Rough Guide to Walks in London & Southeast England*, and has travelled around the world on photography assignments.

Additional Photography Rough Guides/Helena Smith, Kim Sayer, Matthew Ward
Cartography This book contains Ordnance Survey data © Crown copyright and database right 2010
Fact Checker Jennifer Radice

At DK INDIA
Managing Editor Aruna Ghose
Editorial Manager Sheeba Bhatnagar
Design Manager Kavita Saha
Project Editors Shikha Kulkarni, Diya Kohli
Project Designer Shruti Singhi
Assistant Cartographic Manager Suresh Kumar
Cartographer Subhashree Bharati
Senior Picture Research Coordinator Taiyaba Khatoon
Picture Researcher Shweta Andrews, Sumita Khatwani
DTP Designers Azeem Siddiqui, Rakesh Pal
Proofreader and Indexer Andy Kulkarni

At DK LONDON
Publisher Douglas Amrine
List Manager Julie Oughton
Design Manager Mabel Chan
Senior Editor Sadie Smith
Designer Tracy Smith
Cartographic Editor Stuart James
Picture Research Assistant Marta Bescós
Additional Cartography John Plumer
DTP Operator Jason Little
Production Controller Erika Pepe

Revisions Team Caroline Elliker. Kathryn Evans, Carly Madden, Andrea Pinnington, Conrad Van Dyk

The Publisher would like to thank Frances Lincoln Publishers for their kind permission to reproduce quotations from the works of Alfred Wainwright: (Page 22) *The Pictorial Guides: The Western Fells* (50th Anniversary Edition) Book Seven (A Pictorial Guide to the Lakeland Fells): © The Estate of A. Wainwright, 2007 (Page 78) *The Central Fells* (50th Anniversary Edition): Book Three © The Estate of A. Wainwright, 2007.

Picture Credits
a=above; b=below/bottom; c=centre; l=left; r=right; t=top

Photography Permissions
Dorling Kindersley would like to thank the following for their assistance and kind permission to photograph at their establishments:

Abbot Hall Art Gallery; Blackwell, The Arts & Crafts House; Brantwood; Brewery Arts Center; The Brown Horse Inn; Cars of the Stars; Castlegate House Gallery; The Cumberland Pencil Museum; Dalemain Mansion & Historic Gardens; The Dove Cottage; Fair Rigg; Gilpin Hotel & Lake House; Grasmere Independent Hostel; Hawkshead Grammar School; High Fold Guesthouse; Jumble Room; Keswick Museum and Art Gallery; The Lakeland Arts Trust 2009; Laurel and Hardy Museum; Low Sizergh Barn; Lucy's of Ambleside; Miller Howe; Museum of Lakeland Life & Industry; Northern Light Gallery; The Old Dungeon Ghyll Hotel; Patterdale Hostel; Rothay Garden Hotel; Ruskin Museum; Rydal Mount; Sarah Nelson's

Acknowledgments

Gingerbread Shop; St Kentigern; St. Olaf's church; Wasdale Head Inn; The Watermill Inn and Brewery; The Wordsworth Museum & Art Gallery; The World Owl Centre; Yew Tree Barn. Also all the other museums, hotels, restaurants, shops, galleries and other sights too numerous to thank individually.

Works of art have been reproduced with the kind permission of the following copyright holders:
Oval Form, Trezion, 1962-3, Bronze 170 x 119.4 x 104.14cm by Barbara Hepworth © Bowness, Hepworth Estate 66bc.

The publisher would like to thank the following individuals, companies, and picture libraries for their kind permission to reproduce their photographs:
4CORNER IMAGES: SIME/ Massimo Ripani 88-89.

ABBOT HALL ART GALLERY: 40cra; ALAMY IMAGES: Ashley Cooper 43cl, 50tc; Roger Creber 14-15c; Homer Sykes Archive 41cl; North Wind Picture Archives 32bc.

BRATHAY HALL: 116TC.

DAVID R. GODINE, PUBLISHER, INC: 40tl.

MARY EVANS PICTURE LIBRARY: Illustrated London News Ltd 32tl.

MASTERFILE: Robert Harding Images 50b, 51tl.

THE NATIONAL TRUST PHOTO LIBRARY © NTPL: Andrew Butler 4-5; Stephen Robson 62-63.

PHOTOLIBRARY: Britain on View/ David Hunter 1c, /Alan Novelli 93cl, /Dave Porter 83tr, /Andy Stothert 30-31; Japan Travel Bureau 40cb; Loop Images/Kim Kirby 21tr; Kevin Richardson 7bl; Robert Harding Travel 42tc, /James Emmerson 42bl, /Roy Rainford 91b; Still Pictures/Paul Glendell 72-73; PUZZLING PLACE: 28c.

RUFTY TUFTYS: 57tr.

All other images are © Dorling Kindersley. For further information see *www.dkimages.com*